00801772

A LIGHT THAT NEVER GOES OUT

A LIGHT THAT THAT NEVER GOES OUT

A MEMOIR

KEELIN SHANLEY

GILL BOOKS

Gill Books
Hume Avenue
Park West
Dublin 12
www.gillbooks.ie

Gill Books is an imprint of M.H. Gill and Co.

978 07171 89472

Edited by Alison Walsh
Copyedited by Jane Rogers
Proofread by Kristin Jensen
Printed by CPI Group (UK) Ltd, Croydon, CRO 4YY
This book is typeset in 12 on 20pt, Sabon.

The paper used in this book comes from the wood pulp of
managed forests. For every tree felled, at least one tree is
planted, thereby renewing natural resources.

A CIP catalogue record for this book is available from the
British Library.

5 4 3 2 1

For Lucy and Ben

'Remember to look up at the stars and not down at your feet ... Be curious. And however difficult life may seem, there is always something you can do and succeed at. It matters that you don't just give up.'

Stephen Hawking

CONTENTS

INTRODUCTION

THE WAY TO SPRING
JANUARY 2020

I have thought of many titles for this book. *Remembering, Towards the Light, As I Am, Who I Am* ... the list goes on, because how do you sum up a life in a few words? Any life, not just mine. Every one of us is unique and we all take different paths; we face different circumstances, different challenges. Some of us are born with huge advantages; for some, life is a daily struggle. Understanding that has been at the heart of my work as a journalist. It's what motivated me to go out on the streets of Ireland and beyond to ask people to tell me about their lives, to share their stories with me. I'm not Princess Diana, I must add: I'm just a woman – a woman with more than usual curiosity, perhaps – but still, just me.

Like anybody else, my life has had its fair share of losses and gains. I'm a happily married mum of two (amazing!) children. I'm lucky to live in a lovely home with my husband, Conor, with my extended family close by. I have had an exciting, interesting job. I have also faced cancer twice, as well as losing my beloved mum, Orna, to the same disease when she was just sixty-one. I know I'm not unique, I don't pretend that I have all the answers, but I also understand that maybe sharing my experiences, and the way I've coped, might be of some benefit. I hope that you, the reader, will be interested in my stories, but also that you might get something from this book of mine: an insight into the work of a TV journalist, a sense that life is worth living, that family is to be cherished, that hope and joy are part of the everyday.

As I write, I know that I have, at most, months to live. I'm fifty-one years of age and I've had cancer for nine years, stage 4 cancer for three of them. I managed to keep my life running until just last November, when a final throw of the dice in the shape of a promising new therapy failed. I had been diagnosed with breast cancer in 2011 and thought I'd beaten it, but then a niggle in my shoulder in 2016 led to a CT scan, and as soon as I saw it in the imaging room in St Vincent's Hospital, I just knew.

I understood what the odds were the first time I had cancer and they were good: with my kind of breast cancer and after the treatment I'd had, there was every chance I'd live a long and happy life. I *was* living a happy life: I was a mum, a wife, a daughter, a sister, relishing all those roles – struggling to balance them all at times – but grateful for everything I'd been given. I'd had a fantastic career and felt privileged to have seen some of the most exciting and dangerous places in the world and to tell viewers about them, and about the ordinary lives of Irish people. After years of living in the city, I had moved close to the sea and could enjoy the light streaming in through my living room window, the sounds of the seafront in the summer, the smell of salt in the air.

And then, on a cold day at the end of November 2016, I could see it in front of me: the bright pinpoints of cancer in my shoulder lit up on the screen and I understood that it had come back. Nobody had confirmed anything, but in my gut, I knew. I can still remember texting my oncologist, Dr Janice Walshe, that night, asking the kind of questions no doctor wants to answer: 'Is this what I think it is? Should I be as worried as I am?' She was fantastic, said she'd do more tests, would take all the steps that needed to be taken. But that night my phone was silent and I knew what that meant, even though I told myself that everything would be all right.

The call came the following day. I'd gone for a walk along the seafront in Dún Laoghaire with Conor and our black poodle, Dougal; I'd watched him bounce along the granite walkway. Like every parent, I'd had to be persuaded that a dog would be a good thing. Our children, Lucy and Ben, lobbied long and hard. But in the end it was love at first sight. Dougal has brought us such joy as a family, I remember thinking, watching him bark at the sea and sniff the ground. Then my phone rang. Janice just said it straight out. 'Keelin, there is cancer in the bone and there are also multiple spots of cancer in the lungs.' She didn't hold back and she was right – there simply is no other way than to tell the truth. She went on to say, 'I'd like you to come into hospital now so we can do all the tests we need to do.'

It's funny what you can remember about these things: everything is the same and yet everything is completely different. The sea, the path beside it with the seagulls and the discarded paper napkins from Teddy's Ice Cream, the Fish Shack restaurant with its big umbrellas flapping in the breeze, the freighters crossing the bay – everything just seemed so normal. And yet it wasn't at all. It was devastating. Conor and I hugged each other tight and even though I'm not sure if I cried, I know that Conor did. I'd never seen him in tears and at first it was frightening. I wondered if he could see something that I couldn't: what the world would be like for him without me in it. The enormity of it was hard to grasp.

Everyone who knows me would say that I'm a doer, not given to flights of fancy or intro- spection. Conor says, diplomatically, that I'm very 'task-driven'! He would also say that in many ways, the cancer for me has been just another task or project to be chipped away at, to be dealt with as

I've dealt with other challenges in my life – by simply getting on with things. It's not that I'm deliberately minimising my illness or its effects on me, it's simply the way I've chosen to deal with it. A friend said to me once that she thought that the reason I'd managed to stay so upbeat in spite of everything was because I'd chosen to 'walk with' my cancer. I didn't know what she meant at first, but she went on to explain that I didn't let it dominate my daily life. I simply put it to one side, accepted the treatment and got on with the business of living. The first time I had cancer, in 2011, I was working in RTÉ, on *Frontline* and *The Consumer Show*, bald but rocking my wig! Nobody noticed, thankfully, but the point is, this is the way I chose to handle my illness. Not everybody will necessarily want or be able to react in the way I did, but it worked for me. That first time, I made a decision that I wasn't living with cancer. I was going to live without it, in spite of it.

Now, however, walking with my cancer was no longer an option. Once I got that call from Janice, I knew that it was only a matter of time before I was no longer able to do so. I hadn't beaten the odds – they had beaten me. I can still remember waking up in hospital the day after that call, waiting for the tests that go with a diagnosis, and having an unfamiliar feeling that I couldn't identify at first – a kind of hopelessness; suddenly remembering all over again the fact that I had stage 4 breast cancer. I knew there was nothing we could do. There was a twenty per cent survival rate. Most people die with this, I thought. I had never thought that death would come for me, though – nobody ever does, until they are facing it head on.

Still, I fought it. I've always thought that you can get used to the strangest things, and soon that feeling of hopelessness lifted. I've always known that life is finite, but now I had to accept that mine would be more finite than most. So I tackled it as I've tackled so many things in my life – just get on with it and see what happens. Or, as Conor liked to say, 'Let's not panic until we have to.' I knew there was a plan at RTÉ to offer me a job presenting the *Six One News* and I was going to go for it, if they would still give me the chance. It was a nervy discussion to have, and I will always be grateful to them for the outcome. I feel that by taking the job, with the support of my husband and children, I managed to defy the odds for another three years. Three years filled with fun and happiness and the buzz of live television that I love.

People often ask me if I feel angry that my cancer returned. Usually I say, 'Why would I be angry? Why shouldn't it be me?' What it comes down to is luck – that's all that stands between me and somebody else who hasn't got the disease. I know that, even though every day I struggle with the reality that I'm facing death. Sooner rather than later, I will be gone from the world, leaving my family behind me. Mind you, sometimes I do get angry. It might be at some selfish driver cutting me off on the motorway, someone jumping the queue at the supermarket or someone airing conspiracy theories on Twitter and I find myself saying, 'Why couldn't cancer have chosen that eejit instead of me?' But then I turn the page in my head and move on.

Three years down the line, I know that I'm in the last stages of the disease. I spend most of my time in bed or on the sofa, my hair is nearly gone, I have fluid on my lungs and pain in my arm from the PICC line inserted to administer some of the numerous drugs I take every day. My face is getting bloated from steroids. I have a blood clot in my brain and I've half a clot in my leg. I don't think I'm quite there yet, but I know how quickly things can change. If I got a significant infection, I'd have very little resistance to it. And yet, as I write, I'm sure there's a lightening in the winter days, even though it's only January. I think I can see buds coming on the tall linden tree outside my bedroom window (although I might be imagining it). I have always loved to follow that proud tree's progress through the year: to see its branches filling up in the springtime, almost disappearing under the weight of its leaves in summer, then turning again in autumn, the leaves slowly going orange, then falling away.

Now, as I look at my tree, its barren, thin branches are stark against the sky. It's a reminder of what's happening to me. Here am I in my winter phase, but I'd love to see another spring. I'd hate to leave Conor and the children now, when the sky is grey and the weather bleak. I think it would be best to die in springtime, when the air begins to warm and the evenings get brighter and new life is everywhere. That is my wish now. I may not get it, but I know that I'll keep trying.

When she heard of my cancer, my good friend and fellow journalist Niamh O'Connor, who is now Deputy Director of Content at RTÉ, took a trip to the archives at the station to dig out old programmes of mine. I think the purpose was to entertain and divert me, to make me laugh at old hairstyles and make-up, at my first nervous attempts to talk to camera. But as I looked at documentaries set in dingy corners of Dublin, or equally gritty encounters in far-flung places, I remembered the person I had been: driven, energetic, up for a laugh and committed to telling stories. And I realised that I still am that person, in spite of everything. In spite of the wig, the scarves, the IV lines, the tests, I am still Keelin Shanley: mum, wife, news presenter, daughter, sister, stepdaughter – I am all of those things.

And that's why I decided to write this book: to remind me of who I am, and to leave those who love me something to hold on to. No child should have to lose a mother, but Lucy and Ben will, and they will grieve, I know. Conor will have to carry on without me. My father and stepmum, my brothers and sisters too. I don't know if it sounds egotistical, but I want to leave a little piece of myself behind for them so that I live on in some way in their memories, as well as in who they are. But I've also come to understand that this book is for other people too. For the people whose stories I've helped to tell; the people I've worked with; and the people who might be dealing with cancer and just want to know that someone understands what they're going through.

Everyone wants to think that their life has significance, has meaning. I'm no different, except that I have visual evidence of the years that have passed, markers of what I did out there in the world. As I sit here on my sofa, looking back at the work that I've done has comforted me. No matter how embarrassing or how illuminating these records are, I've watched them and seen myself grow into the woman I am now. Of course, I'm still wondering about my death. I'm still asking myself the same big questions about life and understanding that for many of them, there are no answers. But in the process of writing this book, I've made my peace with that. Really, all I can say to you is: this is who I am.

CHAPTER I

COMING HOME
JULY 2019

The car pulls up in front of our house and the first thing I notice is how my tree has lost the first bright-green lushness of early summer. Now the leaves are dusty and the heat has made them droop slightly.

For some reason, as we park I'm suddenly struck with a memory of me pushing Lucy down the street in her pram when she was a baby, her little eyes focused on the bare branches of the tree waving above her in the wind, laughing away to herself.

It's probably not an accurate one – Lucy probably couldn't see that far aged two months – but memory can be a funny thing, giving certain times a crystal clarity while the day-to-day gets lost in the blur of business and activity.

I have come home to Dublin after three long weeks in America. I went in search of a miracle, I suppose. I had put myself forward for a new immuno-therapy trial being run by Dr Steven A. Rosenberg at the National Cancer Institute in the famous National Institutes for Health (NIH) in Bethesda, Maryland. I had only managed to get in front of the medical team because I was born in the US. After twenty-one days going in and out of their vast campus, being poked and prodded, scanned and operated on, I'm home. It was an exhausting experience, partly because I'd had to stop all cancer treatment a few weeks previously and partly because of the blur of airport-apartment-shuttle-hospital-repeat that seemed to whizz by over the three weeks.

America was my last hope. I had read on the BBC News website about a revolutionary treatment, where an American woman's stage 4 breast cancer had been reversed; her own immune system had been harnessed to fight the cancer cells. Obviously it's a bit more complicated than that, but that was the treatment in a nutshell. It was at an early stage, but all I could think was, I need to get on that trial. After two years of chemotherapy and various other drugs my options were narrowing by the day, but the prospect of the trial kept me going, gave me something to fight for. It was a gruelling three weeks of tests; everything from MRI scans to a procedure called apheresis, where they removed huge quantities of my blood over a couple of hours, extracted a portion of it, and then transfused the rest back into my body again. I also had surgery on my lungs to extract cancerous tissue. It was fascinating and I willingly submitted to it all to give myself that fighting chance of survival.

I open the car door and Conor helps me out. I'm feeling pretty ragged, even though I slept for the whole flight home. I stand on the footpath in front of the house and take a deep breath of salty air, looking up at the tree's thick green leaves, ears pricked for the noise of the kids playing in the little park in the middle of our square. I climb the steps on shaky legs to the front door and ring the doorbell. A sound of barking comes from deep within the house and then footsteps shuffle up the long hall to the front door. It opens and Dougal bounces out to say hello, followed by Ben and Lucy. I give them both a tight squeeze, inhaling the scents of shampoo and fresh air, trying not to cry on them. At eleven and thirteen, Ben and Lucy are at the stage where they often regard their parents as a bit of an embarrassment, so hugs and kisses are all the more rare and so precious to me.

I can't believe how much I've missed them. I've never been away from them for so long, even when I was filming around the world. I don't want to let either of them go. Of course, I know that they've been just fine, thanks to my little sister Emma and her husband Jamie, who had so kindly moved in to look after them both, along with their own three children. For years now, they have had their own gang, called the Famous Five, and they all had a ball together while we were away, running around the park in the summer light, climbing trees and only coming in as it got dark. There's something I love about the sounds of summer: the rustling of the trees, the *thwock* of tennis balls on rackets as impromptu games are played in the park, the wood pigeons cooing – it's all light and warmth and hope. Normally it would be heaven, but after the last three weeks, I'm utterly exhausted. I can't believe that until just one month ago, I was still working, reading the *Six One News* with my co-host and friend Caitríona Perry. We had developed such a close partnership, one of us rarely seen without the other, and I miss her hugely. It seems as if a whole lifetime has passed in a moment. I can still see myself on my last day at work, applying fake tan to my legs as I cradled my mobile phone under my chin, asking questions as background for the headline news of the day. There's no greater distraction from the annoyances of cancer than the buzz of live TV.

It wasn't my choice to stop working at this point: my boss, and great friend, on the *Six One News*, Hilary McGouran, was one of the few people with whom I'd shared my plans to go to the States and she had urged me to take it easy. In fairness, this came after I'd had to interrupt a meeting with her, just before I was due on air, in order to vomit in her office bin. She was very nice about it; however, she told me I needed to conserve my energy, as I had a long road ahead of me in the US. But if I'd had my way, I would have kept going. Work and RTÉ were my safe place; the corridors had become so familiar to me after twenty-odd years, running up and down the stairs to the newsroom from my desk to update a story or embark on a bit of research. To me, RTÉ was home and family – in a different way from my real home and family, but so important nonetheless. I think I also saw work as a life raft of sorts, to which I could cling when illness made everything else in the world seem unpredictable. It had kept me going through my first diagnosis of breast cancer in 2011, and I had been working in the newsroom for two solid years when I was told my cancer had returned in 2016. Without the work, I felt I just wouldn't be me.

Now, I want to take to the bed and lie there, watching *The Sopranos*, which has kept me going throughout this new phase of the cancer. I had forgotten what a fantastic show it was, and somehow Tony and Carmela Soprano's travails make me forget my own for a bit. But I'm desperate to catch up with the children, to ask them what's been going on in their lives for the long weeks that I've been away. They aren't as desperate as me, however: their ability to live in the present never ceases to amaze me.

Having said the most perfunctory of hellos, they're back out in the park playing a game of rounders and their voices drift up to me three floors above, happy and bright, as I sit on my bed, summer sun streaming in through the windows. For them, each day is a new beginning, and I can't help envying this ability while I sit, suitcase beside me, willing myself to unpack, as Conor clatters around downstairs making tea. For a moment, I let myself dwell on what life might be like for them all when I die ... But just for a moment, because I know that I can't let the darkness take hold, not even for a second. If I slip, I know that everyone else will too, so I tell myself to stay positive. The trip to the US has been a last roll of the dice. Being a relatively new treatment, nothing is guaranteed. I don't even know whether or not I'll be a successful candidate – maybe the blood cells they've harvested won't grow as they need to. So now, the waiting begins. The waiting and the hope for that miracle.

❧

While I was away, Niamh had been true to her plans to offer me a diversion, digging out some more clips of my TV work to watch, and I decide to leave the unpacking for a while and take a look, Dougal beside me, happily guarding his mistress once more – while also snoring lightly. I lift the remote control, resting my head on a pillow as I let myself succumb to how I feel, just for a few minutes. Every single bit of me hurts, from my feet, which feel like two giant boats on the end of my legs, to the top of my head, my muscles wearing from the effort of carrying myself, even with Conor's help and on a walking stick, through airports and hospital corridors. I rub Dougal's shaggy fur and try to relax, flicking on the TV, watching the *Prime Time* logo emerge on the screen and, with it, a flood of memories.

I'm just in the corner of the shot, my dark brown hair long and curly. A young man appears on screen, talking to me. 'This queer pulled in and we bet lumps out of him. He was in bits on the ground – his face was all busted up and we took his car.' David (not his real name) was only fifteen, but he was already in Trinity House, one of the most secure places in the country for young boys who offend. It was so casual the way he described beating up a young gay man but his seeming indifference to what he'd done wasn't new to me. I'd been working on *Prime Time* for a couple of years by then and had seen the dark side of Irish society any number of times. That didn't make it any less heartbreaking, even though, being a rookie investigative reporter, I'm not sure I fully understood the lives of people who weren't like me. I wanted to, though. I've always been curious about how other people live, ever since childhood, when my mother would welcome the children from a neighbouring group home in Greystones into the house for squash and biscuits. I really wanted to hear their stories, even if, back then, I was afraid to ask. But I learned: clambering in and out of squats, sitting in the back of garda cars during chases, chatting with homeless people on the boardwalk in a chilly spring gale – it was all part of a day's work as a documentary reporter. It could be grim, and sometimes it was hard not to give in to the hopelessness I saw around me. But it was also unpredictable and exciting. I was a young woman on a mission and thinking about that young woman makes me smile.

My interest in social injustice, not to mention my work ethic, came from my parents, Derry and

Orna. Dad was, and is, a driven character who loved his job and who came across people from all walks of life while running the famous Dental Hospital at Trinity College Dublin. Mum was a physiotherapist who worked part time while raising the five of us *and* getting involved as a volunteer with the anti-apartheid movement in Ireland. I'm the eldest, followed by Muireann, Eoin, Emma and Niamh. Mum and Dad would drill into us that we were the lucky ones – we'd had every advantage in life – and they were right. (Apart from the lack of sweets. Having a dad who's a dentist could be a real pain sometimes.) Life in the eighties wasn't easy for anyone, but we had it better than most. We may not have had tons of cash – nobody did in those days – but we did have the best education money could buy, willing and interested parents, and we lived in a seaside suburb of Dublin.

It has often been hard to square this stable, financially secure upbringing with the lives of some of the young boys I met for the documentary. I remember one little fellow, a thirteen-year-old, rubbing his eyes outside the Children's Court, because he'd been out joyriding all night. He looked like a baby, telling me about stealing cars and holding up newsagents, lifting the till off the counter as soon as the shopkeeper's back was turned. I didn't have children at the time, but if my son Ben was looking at me like that, exhausted, I'd say, 'You need to go to bed.' This little fellow had nobody to tell him that, as far as I could see. During my time at the court, only one child turned up with his mother – a nice woman at the end of her tether, unable to control her son, but equally unable to get him the help he badly needed. That was the depressing story at the time, and many of these boys would most likely progress to the adult prison system and ultimately Mountjoy. It's the same cycle that persists today.

Dad was from a working-class background too, one of seven children who grew up in a small house in Crumlin. But his dad was a civil servant and his mother, my Nana, pushed her kids, drove them to get an education and to better themselves, as you could in those days, when social mobility was easier than it is now. All of them did well and Dad chose dentistry as a profession, at which he excelled, ending his working life as Dean of the Faculty of Health Sciences in TCD. He'd lived in America, where I was born, then Liverpool, where I spent my early years, before returning to Dublin. Setting up the Dental Hospital was his lifelong ambition and I remember every Budget day he would sit down and say, 'Is there going to be any money for the Dental Hospital?' Years later, when I ended up presenting the Budget with Bryan Dobson, as I followed that day's facts and figures I'd always wonder who might be out there, waiting for a crucial number that would make all the difference to their lives. I'd always sat through it in childhood, not really understanding the impact of three pence on a gallon of petrol or an increase in the rate of income tax.

Dad used to work incredibly hard. He was really engaged by his work and put so much into it. I was often reminded of him during my own late nights working in the edit suite, obsessively honing the report so that it was as good as it could be. I have always recognised the fantastic influence he has had on me. His humour, his analytical tendencies, his tenacity. When we were growing up, he always took life at a run, never a walk, racing to the Dart, outpacing me as I hurried to get onto the same train to secondary school at Loreto on the Green. Even now, in his seventies, with Parkinson's, he hasn't slowed down all that much: he makes sure to get his ten thousand steps in every day. It wasn't until my twenties that I really *got* his wry, spiky view on things and we always got on so well together – even when we drove each other mad. He is so attentive, generous and kind.

Mum, Orna, was a shy character, probably in part due to her stutter, which affected her deeply. The fact that she married someone called Shanley – 'sh' being one of the sounds she particularly got stuck on – was unfortunate and I'm ashamed to say that, like many kids, we teased her about it – but we also answered the phone to save her the embarrassment of trying to say her name. I think I've inherited Mum's shyness. I know it might seem kind of ironic to say this, given that I ended up in the public arena, but I am far more comfortable asking the questions than answering them – it's not about me, it's about the story. Frankly, I don't really find myself that interesting! Perhaps a book about myself isn't the best forum to admit this, but I feel that the experiences I've had, personally and professionally, must count for something. I've always had it in my head that there's a book in what I've been through: the way Irish society works, who gets listened to and who doesn't and why. I always tried to be non-judgemental, to be an interested observer, asking questions because I wanted to know the answers. It's unbelievable the effect that could have on people – young criminals, gangsters, the homeless – they would just talk to me because I was listening to their story. I wasn't trying to be Mother Teresa, I hasten to add, I was just a reporter, but I found it hugely satisfying to tell the stories of people who didn't usually get listened to.

Journalism wasn't a lifelong passion for me, even if I always had a strong interest in social issues. I come from a long line of medics, so that world seemed the natural place for me, in spite of my tendency to be easily distracted. I was a bright child, but a bit wayward, a bit of a messer in school, where I'd get up to scrapes, for want of a better word, but didn't really do anything that bad. I did meet an old friend not so long ago who reminded me of my daily visits to the head nun's office in secondary school. 'Will Keelin Shanley please go to the principal's office?' was a regular refrain, apparently. Can't imagine why ... I was one of the youngest in my class, so maybe that's why I was so high-spirited. I don't know, but I think that once I channelled that energy into my job at *Prime Time*, it gave me a real focus.

I can remember that as we spoke to these young boys, we were aware of just how badly damaged their lives were and how difficult it would be to turn things around. As Father Peter McVerry said at the beginning of the programme, 'In the city, from the time some of these children are baptised, you can tell which of them is going to end up in Mountjoy.' That's a stunning indictment of the inability of our health and social services, as well as the courts, to control some of these youngsters.

We went to one deprived area of Dublin to see a gang of twelve- to seventeen-year-olds just hanging around. Two of them told us about the robbery of €3,500 they'd carried out the previous week. They'd already spent the money on clothes and hash, but, touchingly, one of them had given his mother €300. When I asked what would happen to them now, one of them said cheerfully, 'I'll be locked up, because I have about fifty convictions.' They had a little den in a boarded-up flat, filled with their stashes of hash and cash, which they were happy to show us. Later that night, we visited another group of young men who were standing around a bonfire. Again, they were happy to show us the burned-out mopeds strewn around the place as a stolen car whizzed by, driven by other youngsters. They loved being chased by the guards, and one of them had served three months in St Patrick's Institution for young offenders. 'It's like home,' he explained.

We also spent a night with the gardaí in north inner-city Dublin, patrolling the streets as one of them explained that they could devote all of their time to youngsters, such was the level of trouble, but they just didn't have it to spare. A core of eight to ten kids from the area were responsible for most of the crime, be it stealing cars, burning them out, joyriding or shoplifting. One car chase ended with the kids getting away and, later that week, we met them gathered around a Hallowe'en bonfire. 'We were fast on our feet,' the boy explained when we asked him how he'd managed to avoid being caught. 'The thrill you get out of it is inhuman,' he explained.

It was hard not to get emotionally involved, even though every bone in my journalist's body told me that it wasn't my job. For instance, there was a young Traveller, 'Stephen', who we all took a real shine to. He had brains to burn and was a real live wire, but with both parents unable to look after him, he had become a street kid. Even then, his ability to lead was clear. He was the voice of a group of young boys who'd hang out in Dr Quirkey's arcade on O'Connell Street playing the slot machines, and he'd become a kind of unofficial fixer for us, travelling around in our van, gaining access to squats around the city. We didn't encourage him to do this, needless to say, but he knew every nook and cranny of the city and he was a huge help to us in finding people we could talk to about drugs and crime. However, he found it incredibly hard to control his anger and it kept getting the better of him. We did everything we could to help, finding him a slot at a local GAA club to use his clear athletic abilities, but his temper won out and he soon drifted away. Some months later I got a call to say that he was in prison, and then one day I ran into him on Grafton Street. I couldn't believe how he'd changed. His face was grey and his cheeks were hollow. He'd drifted on to heroin and when he asked me for spare change, I knew how hard that was for him to do. Never once in all the time I'd known him had he asked me for anything. He died two weeks later.

∽ℰ∼

Now, as I lie on my bed, I can't help wondering about the different paths our lives take. We were all babies once, loved by our parents. The only thing that separates us from each other is circumstance. I wonder what's happened to the young boys in that programme. Who lived and who died, who went to prison and who managed to escape to a better life? I'm struck by how different life can be for people just a few streets away from where we live. Whole lives lived out in the shadow of poverty. I'm glad I spoke for them, in my own small way. Thinking of the problems of the world can often make us feel hopeless, but at least I managed to chip away at one or two, I think to myself as I lie there. Then Dougal shuffles on the bed beside me and I'm back in the room once more. The sun is sinking now, shining through the leaves of my tree, their shadows dancing on the carpet. The window is open and a gentle breeze cools the air. As I lie there, feeling my body truly relax for the first time in weeks, I think, well, I did my best.

CHAPTER 2

A TIME OF FIRSTS
JULY 2019

'm sitting in a wobbly boat on the Shannon,
listening to the rain thunder down outside. Inside
the cabin of the cruiser, we've just finished playing
cards at the fold-out kitchen table, drinking red
lemonade and eating Tayto crisps. A GAA match
is blasting from the little transistor radio on the
kitchen shelf. Welcome to the 1950s, I laugh to
myself, looking at Ben and Lucy as they squabble
over who won the latest round of gin rummy. In
my own childhood, summers were spent in windy

caravan parks as Dad tried to raise a tent the size of a circus big top that would fit all seven of us inside. It was all sandy sandwiches in my day, even if we were lucky enough to have gone abroad once or twice. A campsite in France was the height of sophistication as far as we were concerned.

Mum and Dad were great outdoorsy people, in the way so many Irish people were at the time, and we had lots of outings to lakes and rivers, fishing expeditions which would end in the catching of no fish, but the welcome sizzle of sausages on a pan on top of a Calor camping stove. On one occasion we forgot our fishing rods, so Dad said, 'Orna, take off your tights there and we'll make up a rig.' Sure enough, Mum removed her brown tights and they were transformed into a rather odd-looking fishing net! We didn't catch anything, I hasten to add.

I feel incredibly lucky to have had a golden childhood, full of laughter and fun, and I'm well aware that I am incredibly fortunate. I always tell people that I've had a wonderful life, and it's true: I have. I think that's what helped me to see cancer as a blip, a mountain to be climbed to coast down the other side. Now, as I wait for results of the tests from the States, I can't help wondering if I can do it all again.

My first encounter with breast cancer came on 25 February 2011. I knew that I had an appointment at the breast clinic at St Vincent's Hospital that morning, but quite honestly, I hadn't given it much thought. Yes, I had found a lump and had been referred by my GP, but with the general election in full swing, in the teeth of a recession and with two small children to mind, I'd put any niggling concerns to one side. I was so unconcerned that I simply strolled up from the office to the hospital by myself and waited for my X-ray, then an ultrasound, along with a waiting room full of worried people.

It was the ultrasound that stopped me in my tracks. The radiologist was lovely and we'd been chatting away about children and the impossibility of getting them into oversubscribed primary schools when she stopped pushing the wand around my left breast and said, 'Keelin, I just have to say, I'd be a little concerned about this.' Oh. My heart stopped, but immediately my brain started whirring. How was I going to tell Conor? How was I going to throw this bomb into our lives? And the second thought was, Who is going to mind my children? They were only two and four at the time. Cancer is such a shocking word to hear and of course I thought, I'm going to die. That's what anybody thinks when they get a diagnosis like that. And I am dying now, but I know that I am the exception, rather than the rule, when it comes to breast cancer.

And then I went back to work! I simply had no idea what to do, so I spent the rest of the day on autopilot, completely dazed. I've always found work to be a great distraction, but even I couldn't cope with it right then. All my certainties about life changed in that one moment. I was no longer in charge of it, able to do with it what I liked. Now my body had taken control. I had been due to cover the Carlow–Kilkenny election count that evening, but Conor simply said, 'Let's get away for a bit. We could try Kelly's?' And so we went to the lovely Kelly's Hotel in Wexford; Conor, the kids and myself. We had never been before but had heard so much about the place, and I have to say it was the perfect escape from it all. We ate ourselves silly at breakfast, elevenses, lunch, afternoon tea and dinner. We went for long walks on the beach and played, interminably, with the kids in the pool. Conor and I even managed a few goes in the outdoor hot tub. It was bliss. I managed to forget about the biopsy results I'd be getting the following week; the meeting that I would have with a surgeon to talk about the diagnosis. It was all a foreign country and I wasn't prepared to venture there just yet.

The fact that I had the most common type of breast cancer, invasive ductal carcinoma, was confirmed the following week. It's a terrifying description for what nowadays is manageable for most women – and indeed some men. I had a two-centimetre tumour, surrounded by eight centimetres of pre-cancerous tissue, Denis Evoy, the breast surgeon, told me. I had no idea what that meant until he added that a mastectomy would be needed, followed by chemotherapy, then radiotherapy. I wasn't really able to take it in, all the talk of tumour grades and hormone receptors; it was as if Mr Evoy had suddenly begun to talk in a foreign language. I left the room, dazed, leaflets in my hand to help me understand my diagnosis, my eyes scanning the room, which was filled with women like me. As I stood there a woman came out of another room, sobbing, but I simply felt frozen, unable to react.

I can still remember the lovely Breast Care nurse trying to simplify it all for me: 'It's going to be a tough year, but then you'll be fine.' Okay, I thought, that's what I'll do. I'll face this tough year and, at the end of it, I'll be well. And in the meantime, I would do anything I could to fight it. If they had to cut off a leg, well, I'd just keep on going on my remaining one. Survival was my driving force. I just wanted to be alive: for me, obviously, but mostly for my family, for Conor and the children.

Telling people was the hardest part, though, looking at the shock on their faces as I revealed my news, over and over again, trying to comfort them, telling them what I believed, that I'd be fine. Telling Dad was the hardest of all, because of Mum. She had died at only sixty-one and he'd been devastated. When I got the diagnosis, he was in America at a big conference and I waited until he'd returned to break the news because I knew that otherwise he'd never have gone. I felt the burden of telling him keenly – I knew that he'd be stoic, because that's Dad, but I also knew that the news would be hard to bear.

Conor and I decided not to tell the kids every-thing. After all, they were so young and to them the word 'cancer' had no meaning. We simply told them that I had a sore lump and that the doctors were going to take it out, then give me medicine to make me better. Their incomprehension was a relief and a worry at the same time. I was telling them things that no two- and four-year-old should have to hear. I knew that their little lives would go on as usual, but the enormity of what was going on in the background would make everything different somehow. My cancer has been present throughout their whole lives now, so I've done everything I can to make things 'normal', so that they can have a childhood. And if they wanted to try on my wig – which I'd leave beside the front door in case of callers – so what? To them, it was just dress-up and I thanked God for their innocence.

Telling them the second time was so much harder as they had begun to understand the unpre-dictability of life – that things could just happen and would sweep away any certainties they'd had, but I'll come to that.

I got through the year and as the nurse had predicted, it was tough. My mastectomy was followed by six weeks of recovery. Then I got an infection, which took me a while to overcome. Then came the chemo, four three-weekly cycles, with the nausea and everything that came with it. I was to start filming a new series of *The Consumer Show* and I managed to do it because filming was on a Tuesday, and thanks to the fact that my chemo was on a Monday, the steroids that they administered to help with the nausea and the tiredness were still in my system, so my energy levels were up. My hairdresser, Helga, was also a huge help, taking time out of her day off to come wig shopping with me, cutting the wig we ended up choosing into a style that resembled my own. Conor says that I should call this book *Getting on with It*, because I did. Cancer, at the time, was not a death sentence for me: it was a challenge I had to overcome by taking each hurdle as it presented itself.

In 2013, I was interviewed by Ryan Tubridy on the *Late, Late Show* for Daffodil Day. We talked about wigs and treatment as pictures of me in one of my wigs flashed up on screen. When I got home, Conor said, 'You were a bit blasé about the cancer.' I had no idea what he meant until I watched the interview back and saw myself with my full head of hair, dismissing Ryan's probing questions about how I handled that year, joking about my children wearing the wigs at Hallowe'en, more comfortable talking about the new series of *The Consumer Show* than about mastectomies. But my intention wasn't to make light of things – it was simply to show that people can and do face the 'C' word and overcome it. I am struck by what I say at the end: that we have to remember, people still die of this disease. At the time, I wasn't talking about me – I was talking about the unlucky ten per cent of women for whom the disease will return in five years. I never for one moment thought it would be me.

∽☙∼

Now, as we chug along the Shannon in our little cruiser, I really notice myself being quietly carved off from the foursome. They don't wake me when they get up, with demands for cereal and TV – instead, a cup of tea is quietly placed beside me in the bed and I'm left to wake up while they get the boat ready to go. I know that they're trying to be helpful, but even so, I feel a bit left out, a bit grumpy that I'm no longer able to keep up and be a full part of our little gang of four. I like to think that we've always moved through life like dolphins, in a little pod, and it upsets me to see how that's changing.

The holiday is a compensation for our missed trip to Newport with Emma and the kids after my stay in the States. We'd had it all planned: the holiday home, big enough for all of us, booked for a whole two weeks, and we were going to have an absolute blast, but in the end I'd been too ill to go. After America, I just seemed to crash and burn: I was in pain, my mouth was sore, my hair was falling out in fistfuls and I was dogged by a constant exhaustion. I couldn't pinpoint the source of my problems, it all just seemed … not right. Janice Walshe, my oncologist, was investigating, trying to work out if one of the many drugs I was taking was causing my problems and, if so, which one. One day I arrived in to St Vincent's for treatment and I was incoherent. My mind just wouldn't seem to work and my thoughts were jumbled and rambling. Janice and Brendan Corkery, the palliative care consultant, were concerned. They asked me if I could pinpoint where it was hurting, but frankly, I was too addled. 'I don't

know what's sore and I can't find out and it's just
...' The words wouldn't come. It felt as if everything
was off balance, and the sense of losing control was
terrifying. Maybe this is it, I thought. Maybe this is
what dying feels like. However, Brendan reassured
me. 'We're going to sort it out. Promise.' Brendan
was born to do palliative care and his words soothed
me. An adjustment to my morphine dose later, and
I was feeling much more normal. I wasn't dying, at
least not yet. Even if the going was tough, I'd live to
fight another day.

I felt terribly guilty that the kids were missing
out on the great Newport adventure, which is why
we've booked the Shannon cruise for a few days. The
kids are in heaven, driving the boat and jumping off
into the water, and every night we stop somewhere
and have dinner, big Irish dinners that I can't eat
because of my sore mouth. I'm not in the habit of
feeling sorry for myself, but have to admit to a bit of
self-pity. Just a tiny bit. A little 'What the ...', before I
stop myself. 'Ah, Keelin, will you cop on to yourself.'
My friend Judy Kelly says that I have enough deter-
mination to power through any situation. She calls
it my 'running through walls' personality and it's

a compliment, I know, but I've really needed it recently. I've had to channel that energy that's taken me through live television, ambitious house renovations, being a working mum, a friend, a hopefully reasonable wife to Conor, and devote it instead to this bloody disease.

When the going gets particularly hard, I like to give myself a little boost by booking a break with Conor and the kids. Nothing fancy, just a few days in Ireland, where I can forget about myself for a bit and where we can all be together. Now, as I sip my tea and listen to them rampaging around outside, I can't help wondering what holidays will be like in the future. Being the planner I am, I like to imagine where they might go as a trio. Maybe Greece would be nice, I think: the three of them could ramble around lovely monuments and eat in little tavernas every night – and the distraction would keep them from squabbling! The dynamic will change hugely, I know. They won't have two parents, so they won't be able to play one of us off against the other, or take refuge with one when the other is cross because they've lost something or haven't done their homework. And I think that it also works the other way. When I'm the soft touch, Conor is the disciplinarian, and I wonder if he'll have to soften when I'm gone. We often joke that I indulge them while he attempts to shape their characters, but together we've always found a balance. What now? I think to myself as the water laps against the hull. What will life look like when four becomes three? I suppose I won't know. I do know that Conor will go on without me, and that the kids will grow up and one day will have families of their own: that I will see none of it makes me feel so angry sometimes. What mother doesn't want to see her children go out into the world?

All these thoughts are making me feel a bit stressed, as if I can't quite pull my thoughts together. I lie back against the banquette and close my eyes, listening to the shouts of the children, and a picture of my younger self pops into my head. I've been thinking about her a lot recently, ever since Niamh sent me another couple of clips, a video of my first-ever live TV performance and an early programme looking back at twenty years of U2, in advance of their PopMart tour. I even got to go to Rotterdam to pre-record an intro for a live link-up to the band onstage. I wasn't too nervous, but I couldn't help feeling, 'How did I end up here? ... Oh, look, there's Jo Whiley!' Yes, the BBC had sent over Jo Whiley to do the same intro for them. A brief wave of imposter syndrome ebbed away when her producer told me I could go first because Jo was having trouble memorising her script.

The experience of watching my younger self presenting these various pieces was slightly surreal. There I was, in my scallop-hemmed skirt and jumper and plum-coloured lipstick, my bobbed hairdo and clunky shoes, a very earnest look on my face. After a couple of years hanging around, pitching ideas to producers and generally making a nuisance of myself, I'd at last got a gig with RTÉ as a film reviewer on a lunchtime TV show, aptly enough called *12 to 1*, with Marty Whelan and Ciana Campbell. There was more than a certain amount of bluffing involved, because even though I like movies, I'm no buff – that's Conor's domain. Nevertheless, there I was, bold as brass, reviewing *Short Cuts*, the Robert Altman film. I had to talk for ten minutes with no autocue, so I had to have a fairly good idea of what I was doing – basically, I had more or less learned my script off. I was all set, but as I was speaking, I noticed that the first clip on the monitor bore no resemblance to the film I was talking about. I was utterly thrown because the clips all came out in the wrong order, so I was talking over clips that we should have been listening to and listening to clips with no dialogue in them. It was a disaster, but I had to keep on talking, reacting live on air – 'Well, that's not what you're seeing' as yet another irrelevant clip rolled up on screen. It was mortifying, but somehow I survived it, and that's the funny thing about live TV – it is nerve-racking and things can, and do, go wrong, but I always try to remember that it isn't about me, it's about the viewer. I'm simply the host and it's my job to look after the viewer, to ask the questions they want to ask. In live TV, you take yourself out of the equation, you stop thinking about yourself – about how you're standing, looking, feeling – and focus on who you're talking to. There's a real freedom in that.

As I remember that gauche young girl now, with my whip-smart comments on U2, I think about this book and why I'm writing it, given everything I've said about not wanting to be the subject. For so many years I've just been a conduit for other people, first for those who rarely get listened to in our society, and then for those who do, but who need to explain their decisions to ordinary Irish people. Why am I writing it, I wonder. What is it I feel that I want to say? Is it just a big ego trip or is it simply my journalist's urge to document, to make sense of what I'm going through? Or does it even matter? Perhaps it's because I'm journeying towards the end that I want to take stock, to look back on who I was, and still am, to reflect on what was important to me and how I lived my life, to reassure that gauche young woman that there was so much more ahead and that she was living her life as best she possibly could.

CHAPTER 3

BACK TO EARTH
LATE JULY 2019

We're driving back from Carrick-on-Shannon, where we've left the boat, the kids happy and sunburned after their few days, Conor beside me in the passenger seat. Since my diagnosis he's been learning to drive, with varying degrees of success. He's failed one test, but only on something small, so we're hopeful for the next one. He has to pass, I suppose, because soon my driving days will be over. It'll be strange to see him pull away from the house and drive off to Cuala to drop Lucy to GAA training, or to leave Ben down to the sea to a sailing class. That was always my job, but now it'll be yet another task that falls to Conor. Sometimes I panic at the idea of the new responsibilities he'll have to carry, but then I reassure myself that since my diagnosis, he's been utterly brilliant. I joke that now he knows where the dishwasher tablets are, but in reality, he's been doing everything: looking after me, doing the homework and the school runs, cooking the dinner, and the endless tasks that go with running a home. Our house has no fewer than 56 steps from bottom to top, and Conor spends most of his day running up and down them. He's been a rock-solid, steady presence during my illness, and I don't know what I'd do without him.

We'd known each other for years, Conor and I, before anything romantic happened. I first saw him on Grafton Street when I was fourteen. He was dolled up to the nines as a Goth, and he made quite the impression as he strolled up the street, hair bigger than everyone else's. I was so fascinated by him that I followed him all the way to St Stephen's Green. Even though we were from the same area, and Conor and his friends would come over to mine on Fridays to listen to my three records, our paths didn't really cross again until we left college, when we'd bump into each other in the local pubs. It was a film festival that finally brought us together in our mid-twenties and from then on we've been inseparable. Our personalities gel, Conor being more reflective and me being a bundle of energy, at least until now, when the roles are reversed.

As I drive, my mouth is humming with pain. It's a common side effect of chemo, but this time the usual rinses and dry-mouth treatments haven't worked, and my palate feels red raw and blistered. I need to get something, I decide, to help with the discomfort, heading towards the South Circular Road to my old neighbourhood chemist. I'm exhausted after the drive and the day is hot and sticky. I really don't feel well, I think as the car grinds to a halt in city traffic. I'll get something in the chemist and straight to bed for me when I get home. Conor gets out of the car to nip into the supermarket for dinner while I park beside the chemist and open my door to get out.

The next thing I know, I'm lying on the road, no idea how I got here. I can remember opening the door, putting my foot on the ground and then

... nothing. I'm on a little side road off the South Circular Road, which thankfully doesn't get much traffic, and the tarmac is hot under my back. My head is thumping where I must have hit the ground and the clouds above my head are spinning. I try to push myself up on my elbows, but don't have the strength. From what seems like miles away, I can hear screaming, but I'm not sure where it's coming from. Hot tears are pouring down my face and I can feel the panic rising. Next thing, Lucy's face is hovering over me and she's lifting my head to place a pillow underneath it. Somehow, she manages to do this while screaming in fear. I wish I could help her, soothe her, but I can't seem to open my mouth.

The next thing I see is the face of a young woman. 'I'm a doctor,' she says. 'I'm just going to check you out, okay?' I try to respond, but I'm ashamed to say that I just can't stop blubbing. 'It's the shock,' she says calmly, placing her fingers tenderly on the back of my head. 'You'll need to go to hospital,' she says. 'You'll have a concussion there at least.' By this stage a crowd has gathered around me, heads peering over me. I feel claustrophobic, unable to breathe. I want desperately to get up and back on my feet. At the very least, if I am going to hospital, I want the familiarity of St Vincent's, not St James's, which is actually closer. So instead of calling an ambulance, Conor calls my sister Emma, who has just got home from a holiday in Texas, and she promptly takes us to St Vincent's.

I arrive at Cedar Ward in St Vincent's, my home from home at this stage. But the lovely nurse explains calmly, 'Sorry, but you'll have to be admitted through the Emergency Department, Keelin.' I'm not looking for special treatment, I just want to lie down on a bed and be looked after, as I have been so many times before, and I desperately want to talk to Janice, but the nurse is firm. 'You have a head injury,' she explains gently. 'You need to get it checked out.'

She's right, of course. Emma zooms us around to the Emergency Department, which is packed on a Saturday night and I wait for a cubicle. Conor goes home to the kids and I try to get some sleep.

Twelve hours later, I emerge, bandaged and bruised, armed with the new information that I have a brain clot. Even I have to swear under my breath, 'F**king cancer.' It's a disease that attacks on so many fronts and if the cancer doesn't make me feel bad enough, the treatment that keeps me alive has plenty of side effects to help with that. From the chemo that makes my hair thin to the steroids that make my limbs weak, not to mention the nausea and the indignity of constipation, I now discover that cancer medication makes your blood sticky, and that this is probably what lies behind my brain clot. Now it's time to add blood thinners into the mix of tablets that I take daily. What's more, I now have to wear surgical stockings, which to me seems a bridge too far! If you haven't had the misfortune to wear them, they are bright white elasticated pressure stockings, which turn a lovely shade of grey in the wash. They do help with clots, but they sure don't make you a style icon!

I come home, armed with my pack of tights, which, clot or no clot, I'm determined not to wear. Getting dressed these days is exhausting enough. Who knew, I think, as I sit on the edge of the bed every morning, that elasticated trousers would be such a blessing? Dunnes Stores has been my friend here, providing me with a few pairs with their lovely stretchy waistbands. I'm not a fashion victim, but I doubt I'd wear them if I was in the whole of my health! Instead of the surgical tights, I've compromised by wearing knee-high socks, which give me a bit of support and aren't too offensive. A nice stripy T-shirt and a warm cardigan and I'm good to go. Even in the heat of summer I feel chilly because I don't have as much in the way of fat to insulate me.

I creep around, head swimming after my fall. It's late July now and normally the house would be alive with visitors, but instead it's eerily quiet. I strain for any sound of the kids, or Dougal barking at the world, but instead, there is silence. It makes me sad – Conor and I have always been great entertainers, throwing impromptu dinner parties or lunches on many a weekend, but this summer I just haven't been up to it. In normal summertimes, our favourite thing to do is to have people over with their families at about five o'clock, to sit in the sunroom or out in the back garden if the weather is nice, while a big pot of something cooks on the stove. The kids run off as soon as they arrive and the adults are left to chat in peace. It's blissful. Now I know that there won't be many more of those lazy Sunday afternoons and I chalk up another loss to the enemy.

Life with cancer is filled with losses, and as I ease myself onto the sofa, I wonder if there have been any gains. My mouth is falling apart, my skin is paper thin, I feel sick and sore everywhere, and in addition, I have a lump worthy of a Tom and Jerry cartoon sticking out of my head. Dear me, I think, the state of me! But I've always believed in fighting off the self-pity. I pick up a book to distract myself, but put it down again. Let's concentrate on the wins, I think, not the losses. I close my eyes, faint sounds of the seafront wafting in through the window, then I open them again to take a long, refreshing swig of the elderflower cordial that's been such a lifesaver. I decide that maybe that's why I enjoy looking over the old films of me in the whole of my health, to feel that I'm still connected to that go-getting girl in the scallop-hemmed skirt.

∾

I was such an eejit in the early days of my interviewing, I remember, so cocky and cheeky. But looking back, I think I felt I had to be. It's that old fear that haunts so many of us: the fear that we'll be found out. The thought process is, if I act the part, maybe no one will realise that I haven't a clue what I'm doing. My first ever well-known interviewee was Ken Loach, way back when I was still a film reviewer. I was very green, thinking that I could ask 'searching' questions and get the answers no one else in the world of journalism was getting. The arrogance of it! Ken Loach was a hero of mine, but he wasn't a bit pleased at my probing questions and he got really grumpy with me. The film he was promoting was *Bread and Roses*, about illegal Mexican immigrants; there was some controversy around it as I remember, but I did a really bad job with the interview, pushing and challenging him unnecessarily, when all I needed to say was, 'Tell us about your film.' Lesson Number One: If you're going to ask a controversial question, start with the questions you will absolutely need to get covered, because otherwise, by the time you get to asking them, it's too late: you're no longer the interviewee's friend. It has to be said, though, that sometimes journalists can feel intimidated, as can interviewees, and the way around both situations is to say: 'Listen, this isn't about me, it's about the viewer, about getting the information out. Try to imagine you're talking to … (an intelligent twelve-year-old is the accepted yardstick). He or she should be able to understand what you're saying.'

Most subjects remain resolutely professional, and politicians in particular are well used to being grilled and challenged. It's all part of their job. I remember interviewing the late Brian Lenihan when he was Minister for Children, around 2002. We'd done a *Prime Time* documentary on persistently high levels of child poverty, which at the time was a real issue. (Sadly, that hasn't changed. Things did improve slightly during the Celtic Tiger era, but in 2017, a quarter of a million children still lived below the poverty line.) I asked the questions I had to ask, and at the end of it, when the cameras were turned off, he said, 'God, that was very tough.' He said it with a smile, though, and I knew that there were no hard feelings. As long as you are fair, you can be as tough as you want. Part of that fairness is giving the interviewee time to answer – you ask the question and let them answer it. I had been fair to Lenihan, giving him the time, and there was mutual respect in play. He then gave me a lift home in the ministerial car! He was such a nice man, and I was amused at the state of the Merc's interior, with empty sandwich boxes and papers scattered around the place, evidence of many lunches eaten on the fly.

I think my favourite disaster, though, if that's the right word – it's the one that, every time I think of it, makes me cringe – was my encounter with the late Martin McGuinness. I hadn't been in studio long, following a long career at *Prime Time*, and I was due to interview him. I did my homework and felt thoroughly prepared – I was going to nail this encounter. I double-checked which constituency he represented with a researcher and off I went. He came on air and the first thing I said to him was, 'Martin McGuinness, as the MP representing Foyle ...' Of course, it was Mid-Ulster, not Foyle, and quite rightly, he made mincemeat of me. I had lost the advantage and McGuinness knew it – he speared me and I don't blame him. There was no coming back from it. All I could do was hang my head in shame, slinking off home to lick my wounds, lying awake for most of the night giving out to myself.

Now, RTÉ people will always say 'that was great' after an interview, no matter what. They'll never say it was rubbish! But the next day, when I slunk back into work, what I got from everybody was big, sad faces. I was so mortified. I learned a valuable lesson: always check. Make your own phone calls. That was a very big learning for me in this new world.

I really cut my teeth as an interviewer talking to people on *Prime Time Investigates*, learning the ropes with the amazing team there. Eddie Doyle, my first producer, who is now head of Content Commissioning at BBC Northern Ireland, was a great teacher. His mantra was, 'Let's just do it.' I learned from him the freedom of programme-making: that you could do what you wanted – you could get out there and ask the questions. You didn't need to wait for the story to come to you. You didn't need to make phone calls – you could just get out on the street, go to where the action was, go to where the kids were drinking or where the bonfires were and just pick it up. There were places kids gathered, for food, for sleeping bags, for buses to the night shelters, and all you needed to do was sidle up and say, 'Hello, can I have a word?' Once they'd established that I wasn't a garda, they were happy to chat, and because the street community is relatively small, everyone in it knows what's going on. That was a crucial discovery for me and it was very empowering. The story's not on the phone, it's out there, and it's up to us as journalists to go after it.

But I never thought we'd get into significant trouble in the process. My belief has always been that people are well able to read you and decide whether or not to trust you. And the majority of them do. However, if they decide not to trust you, get out of there quickly. I can still remember driving into Fatima Mansions in Rialto early one morning with Eddie in search of teenagers we'd heard were dealing cocaine. At the time, Eddie had a car that looked like an unmarked garda car, a Ford saloon of some kind, and in we went at five a.m. We couldn't believe it: the place was alive – there were children in the playground! However, as soon as we arrived, the whole circus stopped and they all just looked at us. My heart was in my mouth. I knew that this wasn't good. And then one girl ran up to us and said through the window, 'You've got to get out of here, you look like police.' Cue Eddie screeching to a halt before attempting a three-point turn. Now, Eddie was a terrible driver and a three-point turn quickly became a twenty-nine-point turn as people began to gather, yelling, 'Get out! Get out!' I felt like wrestling the wheel out of Eddie's hand but eventually, with a screeching of tyres, we exited to safety.

However, Conor often jokes that if he asked Eddie who was the ringleader in our many scrapes, he'd say it was me! For one documentary on Ireland's growing cocaine problem, I wanted to see exactly how drugs were passed around clubs in the city, so I decided to go out clubbing myself, complete with a homemade kit to swab pub toilets for any evidence of cocaine. I donned my rubber gloves and out came the cotton buds! I've never been afraid to get my hands dirty if the story demands it. We also disguised a camera within a fake air freshener to scope the loos, which I'm not sure was entirely legal (we did disguise everyone), but it was angled carefully and was certainly effective.

Ireland at the time was in peak Celtic Tiger mode and cocaine was everywhere. I can still remember interviewing a man who was in the building trade about his cocaine use. In the previous year he had spent €35,000 on the drug and had brought himself to the brink of ruin. I asked him, 'Was it worth it?', expecting him to say no, it had destroyed his life. Instead, he replied, 'Every minute of it.' It was such an eye-opener.

I was prepared to do a lot of things in search of a story. Perhaps others might not have taken risks like I did, but I like to think that the same boldness that had got me into trouble in secondary school really helped me to do my job when getting the story was my only goal. I was capable of laser-like focus when needed. Cedric Culleton, cameraman extraordinaire, talked about this recently when he rang to see how I was doing. He reminded me that for one sequence in the cocaine documentary, we were to secretly film in a big club outside the city. I donned a wig, under which I secreted a recording device, and a pair of aviator shades, behind which was hidden a camera. I thought I looked great! Off I went onto the dance floor with my wig and my shades, filming away, until someone yelled, 'Giz a go of your hidden camera, love!' I had been well and truly outed. Nowadays you can hide a camera in a buttonhole, but times were different then.

I remember one squat in particular that I visited with Cedric. We had to get in through a window and I couldn't get up the wall, so he pulled me up and over the barbed wire on the top, snagging Conor's dad's 1970s sheepskin coat in the process. God knows what I looked like, but it was warm! I had yet to discover the expensive wonder of the North Face puffer jacket! However, when we got into the squat, it was so tragic. There was a young fellow from up Drogheda way and I'll never forget how polite he was, high on heroin, answering our questions. He was such a nice kid, so gentle, a middle-class boy who'd developed a heroin problem. Cedric says that the reason he didn't tell us to f*** off was because of my charm. I'm flattered, but I think that really it was because I just gave him the space to talk.

A few days later, the programme went out and even though we'd blacked the boy out, his mother recognised his voice and she rang me and said, 'We're desperate to find him.' It was very tricky. As journalists, we don't reveal our sources, no matter what. This person has trusted you and done the interview and it's our job to protect them. And yet … I could see that that kid was young and rescuable and had only just started into heroin. I talked it all through with the mother and eventually I said,

'I'll tell you how I find these people. These are the streets I know, these are the squats and these are the techniques I use.' I never heard what happened, but she never came back to me and I think she would have if she hadn't found him. I like to think that this was one story that had a happy ending.

Cedric also reminds me of the programme we did on the rash of 'head shops' that had opened in Dublin selling legal drugs that had much the same effects as their illegal counterparts. As part of the programme, we wanted to see what effect this was having on the criminal drug trade. So we went to meet some armed gangsters up a lane in Cabra. They thought it was an 'absolute disgrace' that the government was letting this state of affairs go on and that it was having a major effect on their business. I asked them about other aspects of their job and they told me, quite frankly, about the strain of having to go out on a Friday night, 'ballying up' – donning a balaclava – and knocking on doors to enforce the drug rules with people who weren't obeying them. Matter-of-factly, they discussed beating people who hadn't paid their drug debts, while adding that they found it all a bit stressful. I had never thought of the gangster lifestyle in this way. It had the makings of a great programme and we did a really punchy trailer featuring one of them, in his balaclava, telling me what he got up to. I can still remember inviting him out to RTÉ to view the footage to make sure that he was happy with it, because he got lost at the Shelbourne Hotel on St Stephen's Green. The man had literally never been out of the narrow streets of north inner-city Dublin. When he finally arrived, a tubby little man in a grey tracksuit, I led him through the newsroom and he stopped dead at one point when he spotted one of my colleagues. 'That's bleedin' Anne Doyle!'

He was delighted with the programme and particularly with the trailer, in which he was every bit the gangster. But the next day, hours before the programme went out, I got a phone call. It was him, telling me that I'd better cut him from my film, or he'd find me and shoot me. Word had got out on the street that he was about to feature in a *Prime Time* documentary and he was going to bring some serious heat down on his colleagues. That was the end of that! But it was a fascinating example to me of how important listening is. That, I owe to my mother.

Her stutter meant that she was more comfortable listening than talking. Nobody was asking those gangsters how they felt, and all I had to do was let them talk.

An important tool for that is silence. I'm a talker, there's no doubt about that, but one of the most important things I learned in my work on *Prime Time* was the power of silence. If you wait instead of jumping in with a response, you'll often get the most staggering pieces of information – people fill silence with all kind of confessions, but also with the kind of truths that make you really reflect on life. That's really what I took away from those early, frantic years in television, that listening, not talking, is the number one skill in reporting. For a chatterbox, it was a valuable lesson.

Those years seemed to pass in a blur of seven-day weeks and twenty-four-hour days. I revelled in all of it. I learned so much from seasoned filmmakers like the brilliant, dogged Mary Raftery, who would never bow to authority; and I had great times with my friend Janet Traynor, who is an excellent documentary maker. She taught me a lot about programme-making and always understood the importance of being immersed in your subjects' world. Working together, we would win three IFTAs (Irish Film and Television Awards) for the documentaries we made on cocaine, intellectual disabilities and sex trafficking. You're never in it for the kudos, but it was great over the years to see our hard work get some recognition. It makes you proud.

But in 2000, my life took a different turn. I had met and married Conor at this stage, and just as my career was on the rise, so too was his. One day, he got a call out of the blue from a head-hunter for an ad agency in Paris. They were looking for a senior copywriter to join their team and someone had put Conor's name forward. In what seemed like no time at all, we were off to Paris, to a very different life.

CHAPTER 4

RELEARNING TO SWIM
SEPTEMBER 2019

've never exactly been an athlete, but I've always been full of energy, up early in the day, out and about; and in the summer, I've always been drawn to the sea. Growing up in Monkstown, trips to Seapoint were daily in the summer – first with my mum, and later with teenage friends, looking out for boys. Now, the Forty Foot is my place. Today, Niamh has dropped in to our home in Dún Laoghaire, a towel tucked under her arm, and off we go for a dip. I have to admit I'm a bit of a blow-in among the die-hard Forty-Footers, but since we moved out here I have really taken to it. Sometimes it's just me, Lucy and Ben, sometimes our friends and neighbour Louise Webb and her daughter, also named Lucy, come too.

I'm not one of those swimmers who get in and go thundering out towards the buoy and back. I'm more of one who huffs and puffs on impact, then does a ladylike breaststroke, head well out of the water. But I still love it – it's the freedom of it. There's nothing like stretching out in the cold water, looking at the clouds above my head, the seagulls soaring, a blast of a horn from one of the tankers heading towards Dublin port. What I also love about the Forty Foot is that it's utterly democratic: it doesn't matter what you look like in your togs – people of all shapes and sizes go down there for a swim – and let's face it, nobody's looking!

It's a lovely day, so the Forty Foot is busy, heaving with a mix of locals and people who have driven out of the city for a dip to make the most of the unseasonably warm day. Lucy and Niamh and I pile our clothes on the rocks and tiptoe down the steps to the water. The Forty Foot is always chilly, but I realise as soon as I get in that the cold is taking my breath away in a way it has never done before. As I ease myself into the water, I can feel my throat close as I fight to take a breath and my limbs feel heavy in the water. I begin to panic. Lucy is wonderful and spots my distress immediately. 'Are you okay, Mum?' I don't want to scare her, so I flail around for a bit, then get back out almost immediately. I can't feel my legs, my arms are weak, my breathing shallow. I sit on the rocks wrapped in a towel and look at Lucy and Niamh swimming, splashing around in the water now that they know I'm okay. I suddenly think, It's going to get me. The cancer is really and truly going to get me. Until this point, I've woken every morning thinking, It's not getting me today. I'd feel a surge of triumph that I'd lived to fight another day, but after the gruelling past few weeks, I can't muster my usual enthusiasm for life. I can sense it gradually narrowing, in mind and body, and even though I know the end is some way away yet, I feel the loss of another precious part of my life. I have never realised how much I love the ritual of swimming until now, when the prospect of it is being taken away from me.

No moaning, I tell myself sternly as we walk back home in the late summer evening. If I begin to moan and gripe, I know that my family will begin to worry. I have to hold it together for them. To distract myself, I head upstairs to the sofa, sinking gratefully into its softness. The light that beams in through the living room window is still bright, filling the room with a golden warmth. I've always loved this room. It has the most elaborate wallpaper, a dark-green and gold motif that only works because the room is large and bright, but it always cheers me up. When I think about this house, it always gives me such a jolt of pleasure, this lovely home that we created together. After years of exile, as I like to call it, in the city, we returned to Dún Laoghaire in 2016, and it really felt like coming home. I wonder what it is about us humans that makes us want to return to build our own nests close to where we ourselves were raised. Maybe we're not in charge of our destinies as much as we think we are.

I decide that I need cheering up, so I have a rummage under the bookshelves for the old photo albums I filled with pictures of my time in Paris with Conor. Yes, photo albums were once a thing! I'm so glad I have them to look at. To me, it was a period of transition, a gap between two lives. I had been single, now I was married; we had bought our first home in Rialto, but hadn't really put down roots there. Also, after Conor had steadfastly supported me, I felt it was more than time to be there for his big adventure, working on international advertising business for IBM and Motorola. Somewhere in the back of my mind, I did wonder about stepping away from my career at a relatively early point, but I knew I needed to take this chance with Conor. I reminded myself that I didn't actually have a permanent job at RTÉ at the time, as I was still on contract. Besides, Paris is an offer nobody can refuse!

I can still remember waiting for Conor to emerge from his chat with the firm offering him the job. We'd flown to Paris for the interview and I'd stood under the Arc de Triomphe, watching the traffic whizz by in a frenzy of honking horns, and I'd thought, Wow, this is going to change our lives. Conor hadn't formally been offered the job yet, but my gut told me he would be. Sure enough, he emerged an hour later and said he'd got it. Sometimes life offers you an opportunity and you simply *have* to take it.

At first, the pace of life was very different. Conor was now very busy with work and I wasn't at all. For the first time in years, I had nowhere to be and it was fun, if strange. We began our lives in Batignolles, in the 17th arrondissement. It was a sweet, rather bohemian place, very down to earth, with a certain frisson. I can remember being in the laundrette one evening reading a magazine and a man walked in looking agitated. Then he left. The next thing I knew, there was a loud smash. I looked up from my reading to find that he'd thrown a bike through the window. Our eyes met as I made frantic mental calculations of whether or not he was dangerous. Sensibly, I looked back to the magazine I was reading, and thankfully he ran away.

We were subletting the apartment from a friend, but it was tiny and a temporary stop-gap, so I busied myself finding a new flat. I found a little walk-up, as New Yorkers would put it, a lovely place with shutters and parquet flooring in an area in the east of the city known as République. Nowadays it's quite chic, but then it was somewhat raw and down-at-heel. The streets were constantly thronged with people of all shapes and sizes, buying food from little corner grocery stores run by Tunisian emigrés and whizzing around on Mobylettes, baguettes slung across the handlebars.

French apartments are usually rented without furniture and this place was no different. In spite of the fact that Conor had gone ahead of me and had been there for a while, there was barely a stick of furniture in the place. I couldn't believe it. The only items of furniture were a solitary armchair he'd got in a *brocante*, or flea market, and a futon. He was using a cardboard box as his table and had borrowed some cutlery from work. He had bought a telly, though! There were a number of trips to a certain Scandinavian retailer in search of furniture, including a cooker and fridge. I also had the pleasure of dealing with the famed French bureaucracy, spending hours on the phone to the electricity and gas companies, filling in an endless supply of forms and enduring long queues in search of my Carte de Séjour.

The other thing that I had the dubious pleasure of getting to know was the infamous Paris traffic. Conor had arranged for the use of the company delivery van to move our bags and baggage from

Batignolles to our new home. As he didn't drive at this stage, I drove through insane traffic up to Rue Batignolles, then to Boulevard de Magenta, then back to the agency, which was just off the Champs-Élysées. Teeth gritted, I swerved and lurched through the jumble of honking horns and angry Parisian drivers still thronging the streets, even late on a Friday night. I was reminded of the time our family had gone to France on holiday. We had a caravan, but that didn't seem like too big a challenge to Dad in spite of the homicidal French approach to driving. We ended up stuck on the roundabout at the Arc de Triomphe, circling for what seemed like half an hour as Dad struggled to exit. As part of his contract Conor was to get a company car, but as I narrowly avoided hitting a taxi, I said, 'You know what, I don't think we need that company car. Tell them you'll take the money instead.'

Still, we managed the move and collapsed, exhausted, in our new home. It seems that every Parisian flat comes with a concierge, who is generally a bit of an old bat. Ours was no different. She was Serbian, I recall, and she did her utmost to make our lives hell, complaining bitterly about the fact that we were always putting the wrong rubbish in the wrong bin. Worse, we had a party once and she never let us forget it, wagging a finger at us and barking, 'No parties!' We were terrified until this really nice North African man who lived upstairs said, 'Don't you listen to her. She's all hot air.' It was a relief to know that everyone else was suffering too. I can still remember that party, which was so lively we had to go upstairs to our neighbour the following day with a bottle of wine in apology. He was an older man and said there was no need to apologise because he was deaf.

At times our little block of flats felt like a scene from Hitchcock's *Rear Window*, as we saw and heard our neighbours' lives play out around us. It was fun, if noisy at times. But then so were we. We ignored the concierge as best we could, but when contact couldn't be avoided, I tried a bit of charm. She was obsessed with collecting dolls, the type with the porcelain face and national costume, so every time I went through the airport, I'd have to buy one for her. I still remember getting one with an Irish dancing costume. It worked, because she did come around to us eventually.

What I remember most about my two years in Paris was the change of pace. It was a bit disconcerting at first not to be working all God's hours and I missed my old job. Not long after we moved, a *Prime Time* report I had made with my colleague Eddie Doyle won the inaugural Radharc Award for Documentary, presented by Mary Robinson. It was for one of my favourite, but saddest, pieces of work, about the daily struggles of many people living in St Teresa's Gardens, Dublin 8. But there were compensations, obviously, and I got used to Parisian life after a while. I used to love walking with my little granny trolley to Bastille market every Thursday to buy veg for the week. I discovered that once locals know you are genuinely living in the neighbourhood and not a tourist, they tend to become more friendly. Nonetheless, it still took six months for the frost to thaw at my local bakery. Every single day I would appear for my baguette without much of a reception. Then suddenly in the seventh month they greeted me with a cheery *'Bonjour, Madame!'* as if I was their favourite customer.

Conor and I used to go out a lot in the evenings to music gigs at places such as the now-infamous

Bataclan, which wasn't far away. It was a legend on the Parisian indie scene even then, long before the tragedy of the massacre in 2015. In fact, I think Conor used Paris to draw out my interest in music. We saw the Fun Lovin' Criminals, Tindersticks, Pet Shop Boys, Paul Weller, Air. I also used to prepare fancy picnics which we'd take to the Seine or to the Canal Saint Martin, which runs through the east of the city. At the time it was a bit scruffy, but has since been polished up and is thronged with hipsters. That was where Amélie went skimming stones in the charming film of the same name, which came out while we were there. We watched it in French, just about following proceedings, enjoying the beautiful soundtrack. What started as a quirky indie movie became a worldwide hit thanks to Audrey Tautou's winsome, offbeat charm, and we felt proud to be living in this glorious cinematic city of such variety and colour, filled with eccentric characters, with their mysteries and little stories – even though the *real* Paris was often hard-hearted, grumpy and overcast.

I loved where we lived because it had a bit of edge. It reminded me of the time I'd spent messing around, for want of a better word, in Europe just after college. I'd done a not-very-distinguished degree in biochemistry at Trinity College and wandered off to Bologna with a college friend, for no other reason than to have a bit of an adventure. Our sole motivation for picking Bologna was because the train stopped there and we were so hungry we had to get off and go in search of food. All the hotels in the city were full because of the famous children's book fair and we ended up sleeping in the railway station along with all the drug users. I didn't tell Mum and Dad, needless to say.

I knew that I'd have to make Bologna work for me – I couldn't just call home and ask my parents to rescue me – so I settled down, got a job in a lab at the university and had the time of my life, teaching English and experimenting with desktop publishing, which was all the rage at the time. It was in Bologna that I took my first steps into the new world of media and away from science. I met a community of artists and dreamers and we made elaborate plans for our future and by the time I returned to Dublin, three years later, I had found my path in life.

Paris didn't represent change in that dramatic sense, but there's no doubting that it was a period of transition for me, from being entirely reliant on myself to being in a partnership with somebody else. I had always pretty much followed my own path, but now I was pausing for a moment to make room for Conor and that was new to me. Still, Paris was the most beautiful place in which to do this.

In my romantic imaginings, I had always assumed we'd end up in the Marais, but I'm glad we didn't – it was too touristy. République and its maze of surrounding streets and boulevards was a lot more real and grounded. It was also home to a giant branch of the incomparable Tati. Long before discount stores made their way to Ireland, France had this Aladdin's cave of a shop, which sold everything from dog leads to sailboats and everything in between. I can still remember my joy at finding a charcoal grey woollen twinset for next to nothing there. I snapped it up and wore it proudly, every bit the chic Parisienne.

Of course, because we were living in one of the most beautiful cities in the world, we had a lot of visitors. Mum and Dad came over a couple of times, and on one occasion we went to an amazing wine fair in some huge event space. When we arrived, we were directed to buy a little fold-out trolley and then go around the individual stalls trying different wines before making a final choice. The vignerons each had their own offering with the wines: little bits of sausage or cubes of cheese, or just the nice stump of an old vine to look at. It was all very buzzy and fun and we were possibly a little tiddly by the time we got from one end of the auditorium to the other. We had already bought a few cases at this stage. Then we walked through a door to discover another auditorium, this one twice the size. It was quite a challenge getting our haul home on the Métro in the end!

Our friends in Paris were mostly expats like ourselves. Greg Delaney had been a really glamorous presence in Trinity College when I was there and had since worked for Lynne Franks PR in London. Famously, she was the inspiration for Patsy in *Absolutely Fabulous*, and Greg was great fun. We were both discovering Paris at the same time, as he'd come to the city to join his French partner, and every now and again we'd take off on shopping trips or to drink a glass – or three – of wine on a Tuesday lunchtime. We were like two naughty children sampling our freedom after years of hard work.

We both found part-time jobs in Radio France Internationale, the francophone equivalent of the BBC World Service. The station broadcast to all French territories, but it also had an English language department, run by an Irishman, John Maguire, a really decent man who gave me my break at the station.

On my very first day in the office, I was shown my little cubbyhole and told, 'Right, you'll be on the Djibouti desk.' Introductions made, my colleague wandered off and I was left wondering where exactly Djibouti was. I'm ashamed to say that I had to furtively look it up in a world atlas. I discovered that it is a tiny francophone country on the Horn of Africa, between Eritrea and Somalia. My job was to find news items of interest and also to report on Djiboutian news stories. I learned a lot during my time on the Africa desk. The stories were so interesting and the crew were – mostly! – great. An expat crew is always very varied: sometimes you get on really well with colleagues, and others, you think, are really crazy, but it was a fun place to work. Furthermore, it wasn't taxing, after my seven-day weeks in Dublin. Before heading to Paris, I'd just finished working on that gruelling documentary on life in St Teresa's Gardens, so this couldn't have been any more different. I should add, however, that I also worked on a few editions of *No Frontiers*, the travel show on RTÉ, travelling to Mauritius, Sweden, Madrid and Malaysia. It was fun, but not as exotic as you might think – and there were only so many times I could sit with a big plate of food in front of me and raise a glass to the camera saying, 'Skål!', 'Salud!', etc.

Life in Paris wasn't all Amélie-style picnics and hand-holding walks along the Seine, though. It was a time of unrest in France, and Place de la République, where we lived, was the designated protest zone for all kinds of groups. Farmers, pensioners, right-wingers, left-wingers … they all gathered there to wave placards and register their noisy complaints. But the march against Jean-Marie Le Pen was one of the biggest, maybe *the* biggest, protest that Paris had seen at that time. It was fascinating to have a front-row seat and I filed a number reports for RTÉ Radio 1 on the situation. The Front National party had been on the rise for many years and in 2002, Le Pen came second in the first round of the presidential elections, pushing a now-familiar law-and-order agenda. The centre and left parties were enraged and frightened at the prospect that he might actually win in the next round. A million people across France went on the march, and 400,000 of them passed through République and walked to Place de la Bastille, where the royals had lost their heads during the French Revolution. Late in the afternoon of the march, Conor and I took our place at the back of the crowds. Many people carried placards identifying themselves as Jewish survivors of the Second World War, army veterans, Algerians who remembered allegations of war crimes against Le Pen during the Algerian War. At one point I could hear the sound of engines behind us. I looked around, expecting to see police vehicles, maybe a water cannon, but it was a row of street-cleaning lorries, flanked by cleaners. Paris still needed to be kept clean, regardless of the politics of the day! In the end, Le Pen was defeated in 2002 (Jacques Chirac won), but the National Front, now the National Rally party, under Marine Le Pen, remains a powerful force in France today.

Our stay in Paris wasn't really about journalism for me, however. It was a blissful interlude, I like to think, before getting back to the real business of living. As I look through the photo albums, with their idyllic pictures of the Eiffel Tower twinkling at night and the timeless streetscapes along the Seine, it seems almost like a fairy tale. It wasn't, of course, but it was a special place and a special time in my life. A time when fun and colour took over for a bit, and what's wrong with that? Now I see it for what it was – an experience, a moment to take stock and to enjoy the simple pleasures in life: food, company, beauty, fun. How lucky I was to have experienced that. Sometimes, when I'm feeling very sorry for myself, I think, I'd be living the dream if it wasn't for this bloody cancer. Then I remind myself, I *have* been living the dream. All these happy memories – who could reasonably ask for more?

CHAPTER 5

REASONS TO BE CHEERFUL
OCTOBER 2019

Today is a good day. I begin by looking out my bedroom window to my tree, to see the bright orange leaves just about hanging on the branches. It's beginning the process of getting ready for its winter sleep and I can't help feeling that it's symbolic somehow. Like a tree losing its leaves, I'm losing my hair now, great tufts of it coming loose in my hands. I've always been quite proud of my hair, thick and dark. Even in my forties, I never had to dye it and it's still a natural shade of deep brown.

I'm the envy of my friends, or rather, I was.

I've never been overly concerned about my appearance, which might seem odd considering that, until recently, I've been appearing on national television. I like to think I get away with it because Catherine Manning in the costume department in RTÉ is a wonder. We have a clothing allowance – not an extravagant one, I hasten to add – and she always knows what will suit Caitríona and me. Caitríona loves bright colours and I'm happiest in navy, even if Catherine does try to nudge us gently outside our comfort zone. And viewers are quick to let us know if we've been wearing something unflattering. Mind you, I was highly amused to see a picture of Caitríona and myself recently, following the announcement that we'd be co-anchoring *Six One*, and we'd been stretched! We both looked over six feet tall. Oh, the wonders of Photoshop.

It's a long way from clambering into squats wearing my sturdy puffer jacket – I'd upgraded from Conor's dad's sheepskin at this stage – or wearing my trusty foreign correspondent's uniform of cargo pants and crease-free shirts. Packing that uniform into my suitcase meant that I was off on a big adventure and it was exciting, even though I was heading to some of the toughest places in the world.

I take out the hard drive Niamh sent me the other week and plug it into my laptop. It starts whirring and I wait, listening to the sounds of the children arguing downstairs. I can't imagine what they are squabbling about and I want to tell them to pipe down, but then there's silence. They must have worked it out between them, I think, smiling to myself. Mum always said that rows and disagreements between us children should just be sorted out without any of us telling tales to her. She was right – sometimes being a parent means leaving them to it. My friends have often remarked on how I am as a mother and the picture they paint sometimes surprises me. One of them once told me, only half-jokingly, 'You think your children can do no wrong, Keelin.' That's not actually true, although I'll freely admit that I indulge them more than Conor does. My attitude is, 'just love them, even those times when they get on your nerves'. On the other hand, Conor believes that our job is to prepare them to be people in the world. I believe that process will happen naturally. I just let them be themselves. I've never wanted to mould them, to push them into a shape of my making. They are who they are and it's wonderful.

Suddenly, there I am, in my foreign correspondent's uniform, walking down a village street in Africa, nodding away as a man tells me his story. My hair is straight, in a bob, and as I watch, I find myself unconsciously touching the wisps that escape from the scarf I've knotted around my head. I see myself climbing aboard a rickety plane and looking wistfully out of the window. I look so young! I must have been around thirty-five at the time. It was the year before Lucy was born and I look relaxed, interested, alert. I wonder what it would have been like if I'd known what the future would bring. Perhaps it's silly to think like that, as none of us can see into our future, but it's tempting to look at my younger self through that prism, to see this foreign trip as a time of innocence.

The series was called *Far Away Up Close*, and I made it with producer Kim Bartley for *Prime Time* around 2005/6. Later series would be presented by Liz O'Donnell and, strangely, John Waters. In the series I worked on, we were going to look at the impact of Irish aid on the ground in Honduras, Ethiopia, Liberia, Uganda, Bosnia and Mozambique. It was just before I had Lucy, so I was still able to do long trips overseas, which I knew I wouldn't want to do with a family. As any foreign correspondent will tell you, it's dangerous work: the world isn't a safe place for journalists any more and even though I'm happy to take risks, I knew that these might not be compatible with family life. So I was aware, even as I packed my bags for my first trip to Honduras, that this trip of a lifetime might well be one of my last.

Our first stop was in Honduras, which at the time was in the grip of gang warfare. I hadn't been to that country before, although I did get engaged in Colombia, in 1999. That was frightening in its own special way. Again, Kim Bartley was involved, having talked Conor and myself, and RTÉ colleagues Donogh Diamond and Ken O'Shea, into visiting the country for three weeks. We made for an odd crew but we had a great time, playing cards, drinking mojitos in the bars that lined the walls of the historic old town of Cartagena and fighting off mosquitoes. We had planned on taking a bus around the country, but Kim informed us that that was not a good idea because FARC rebels, who had been fighting a war with the Colombian authorities for more than thirty years, were kidnapping random people, including tourists, to raise money. Our only option was to head to one of the many tropical islands off the northern coast of the country. It was remote and beautiful and Conor was so taken with it we decided to stay the night. The accommodation turned out to be three hammocks under a straw roof, but our hosts fed us fried fish, plantains and rice and we read for a while, watching the red sun sink below the horizon. It wasn't long before we decided to clamber into our hammocks and go to sleep. Conor was tinkering with his minidisc player when suddenly his hammock collapsed and he hit the ground at speed. He screamed in pain, lying in the dirt. Spotting a cockroach running around, I urged him to get up. He did but then collapsed again in a faint, with his eyes rolling back in his head. It was terrifying. Kim ran inside to call for help.

When Conor came to, he was dazed at first, then I came into focus and he said, 'Will you marry me?'

I wasn't prepared for this! At first, I thought it was the concussion talking, so I said, 'Yes, I will marry you, but you have to ask me again properly tomorrow – if you're still alive.' Apparently he'd had it all worked out that night. He was going to get up early, sneak off and write his proposal in the sand, then come and get me and say, 'Let's go for a walk on the beach.' How romantic. The next morning, looking slightly the worse for wear, he repeated his proposal. Once again, I said yes.

◦◦◦

The trip to Honduras was short on romance, but fascinating for many reasons. At the time, the country received €2.4 million in Irish aid per year and had 28 per cent unemployment. The money sent home from America by Honduran emigrants accounted for more than the value of the country's exports, which is startling. However, we knew that statistics wouldn't bring the aid business alive to viewers in Ireland. We needed stories from this country that had been riven by gang violence and where rural poverty had increased drastically because of the crash in coffee prices in the early 2000s. We had heard about a priest, Father La Buda, who had founded clinics to do tattoo removal and decided to follow that lead to the Honduran gangs that were basically fighting for control of the state.

If you are a gang member in Honduras, you have your life story tattooed on your body, specifically on your face. You might be familiar with the teardrop tattoo, signifying that the wearer has murdered someone, but if you look at photos of gang members, you'll see everything from 'Mother' tattoos to elaborate religious icons. You can imagine how hard it must be to get them removed – or, indeed, to free yourself from a gang once you're involved. The gangs control everything in this part of Central America because it's the route up to the US, and thus alive with drugs, guns and gangs. The two main gangs in this area are MS-13, or Mara Salvatrucha, and the 18th Street gang, or 18s. Interestingly, although these two gangs are among the most feared in Central America, they both began in Los Angeles, among immigrants to that city. In the late nineties the US government cracked down on gang members, repatriating many of them to their home countries. Now they're in Nicaragua, they're in Mexico, they're in El Salvador … and they are battling the state for control every day, with Honduras then having the highest murder rate in the world. At the time the state had introduced harsh new anti-gang laws, targeting the wearing of tattoos in particular, which could result in five years in prison.

The gang members were terrifying, it has to be said, but when we met them it was actually very moving. When we got talking to the fellows with the tats, we discovered that some of them were really just boys, but because they'd been marked almost before they learned to read, they'd destroyed themselves, condemned themselves to a life as an outsider in their society, a thug, a killer, a drug dealer. And yet, some of these young men were going to the trouble and the pain of having their tattoos removed with very rudimentary infrared technology, which left considerable scarring, all so that they could begin anew. This was extraordinarily brave in a country where there was little else on offer. As one man told me, 'I want my children to be better than I ever was.'

We began in the capital, Tegucigalpa, which had a very attractive colonial-period centre, surrounded by mountains. You'd think it would be idyllic, but it was incredibly poor, with many people living on steep, steep slopes without proper sanitation or facilities.

They could be accessed by a series of steps cut into the slopes, and they were riddled with gang members. We were forever being warned not to set foot in a particular barrio: 'Don't go up there. So-and-so from MS-13 is sitting out with his men. Don't let him see you.' It was lawless and dangerous, but even here, people were trying to make a difference. A women's group had brought a shoe factory to the area to provide employment and had even built a police station to shame the police into coming into the area to patrol it. They were also providing pre-school education to local children to keep them from going down the road of many youngsters in the area, who worked in the local dump. When we visited, we were struck by the little people scurrying around on mountains of rubbish, dodging trucks and the many cows that, for some reason, were also grazing on the rubbish. One boy as young as eight told me that he'd been working there since the age of six. Of the 1,200 people who worked on that dump, 500 were children.

Nothing had prepared me for the giant prisons that house gang members. I will never forget visiting one of these places – a vision of hell on earth. Kim had filmed in Central America before, co-directing, with

Donnacha Ó Briain, the award-winning documentary *The Revolution Will Not Be Televised*, on Venezuelan president Hugo Chavez, which is really worth a watch. At the time, she admired Chavez's energy and the vision he had for his country. But the dream faded long before he died of cancer in 2013, at the age of 58. Politics is a febrile business in Central America.

Kim was a fantastic guide. Nothing scared her: she would walk into a den of alligators. But even for her, the prison we visited was terrifying. On the outskirts of Tegucigalpa, it housed 3,200 inmates in a building constructed to take half that number. It was divided into MS-13 and the 18s. Each gang ran its side of the prison, divided by a no man's land in the middle, and the guards did not even go in. They just left the gangs to it. When we visited, it was almost like a small town. There were women in there, bustling about with big dinners, and children running around, even chickens. It was extraordinary to see.

The prison guard, with his big, reassuring gun, dumped us cheerfully at the gate and in we went, armed with nothing more than a camera. Two women from Ireland – what better kidnapping victims? I wondered if the Irish government would

pay a ransom for us ... We were surrounded by a
group of MS-13 'soldiers', who brought us right into
the depths of the building for our visit with the chief.
Every single man was masked with tattoos; I had
never seen anything like that in my life. But, believe
it or not, they were very good to us – they offered
us a cup of coffee and did an interview, answering
our questions thoughtfully. They'd obviously decided
that politeness was the best option, but what I saw
was men doing the only thing they knew how in a
society where choices were, at best, limited.

My overall impression of Honduras was of a
country in the grip of a battle between state and
gangland, and life there was on a precipice. The
newspapers were full of stories of kidnappings,
hijackings, murder. It wasn't just the two gangs
fighting against each other; they were also fighting
against the state. My job was simply to report on
what was going on, not to provide political analysis,
but I could see just how polarised Central American
countries could be, and how large the gulf between
rich and poor was. Furthermore, there is very little
truth for people to take on. In Venezuela, Hugo
Chavez was considered the messiah when he first

came to power, but – even though his heart was in the right place – he was giving people what they wanted to hear. The reality was more complex than that. If you want to improve your health service, where is the money coming from? So much there is coming from crime and cartels: they are an economy all of their own, and who can blame the poor for joining their ranks?

Honduras was dangerous and we had to be careful going around. Properly careful – no button-holing ordinary people or climbing in windows for me – but at the same time, it was wildly exciting.

Liberia, our next stop, was fascinating for different reasons. Here was a bona fide 'failed state', a country in complete disarray after fourteen years of war. The infamous Charles Taylor had just gone into exile, leaving a country in chaos, with nobody in charge. It was hard to believe that Liberia had once been a destination for the rich and famous, full of luxury hotels now transformed into makeshift squats for those fleeing war in the countryside, once-full swimming pools now empty. In one hotel, I walked up a huge marble staircase that had once been covered in red carpet, now bare.

Founded by freed American slaves, Liberia still saw itself as being close to America, and UN troops had moved in to restore order, supervising the disarmament of former fighters. They offered $150 for the surrender of a gun, followed by another payment some months later. A huge part of the problem was the army of child soldiers that Taylor had established, some as young as six. They needed to be demobilised and returned to the wider society. I met one little boy, James, aged eleven, who was being rehabilitated in a home for young children. He proudly showed me his maths homework while telling me how he'd been a commander of the SBU – Small Boys Unit. He had done whatever his leaders told him to do, including killing both adults and children. It was astonishing, really, and I can remember another boy boasting, 'Nobody can get me, I'm bulletproof.' What the adult soldiers did was to 'baptise' the children in water, then fire a blank at them. 'See? You're bulletproof.' And the children believed them. When you have a son of your own it is hard not to feel pain thinking about the lives these boys had already had and wonder what kind of place they might have found in the world.

The country was being rebuilt from the ground up, with a new police force being trained by a group of volunteers from police forces all over the world. With unemployment so high, thousands of former soldiers had nothing to do and riots were common. One of these riots erupted while we were there. Hordes of angry young men, eyes wild and glassy, faced off against equally young state soldiers, resulting in the deaths of seven people. When I went out on patrol with a Liberian policeman and his American trainer Eric, the Liberian, Joseph, said, 'You cannot force respect, you somehow have to earn it.' A trip to a depot outside the city, where payments were being made to former combatants, became tense immediately when a crowd of impatient men gathered around the car to complain to Eric and Joseph about how slow the payments were in coming.

Later, I went out on patrol with a group of twenty Irish soldiers in the lush Liberian countryside. Ably led by Orla, they were chatting to the locals, none of whom would admit to having been combatants. The presence of gold chains or other forms of wealth showed that they probably had been. The Irish army was in Liberia, along with Swedish, Pakistani and

Bangladeshi forces, to keep the peace and to cement relations with the local communities. The soldiers I met were hugely impressive on the ground: it was real hearts-and-minds work and I could see the Irish were good at it.

One day, Kim and I accompanied UN soldiers on a helicopter upcountry to distribute food and supplies to locals and to other UN camps. It was an airborne delivery service, dropping off rice to the Bangladeshi camp, water to a local village and so on. But as it grew dark, we became nervous that we wouldn't get back to Camp Clara in Monrovia. So the decision was made to deposit us for the night at the Pakistani army camp in the middle of nowhere. They were lovely to us, so cordial and welcoming, but it was all a bit awkward, with five hundred of them and only two of us, me and Kim. The general in charge of the camp looked like something from an old film, hair oiled back, terribly handsome and very military. The Pakistani army is based on the British army system, so it was all 'hop to' and that kind of thing. We worked hard to keep a straight face. They looked after us so well, though, feeding us, then putting on a video for our entertainment, which made us both giggle, because it was quite racy. It was like *Die Hard* with a bit more sex thrown in and we could only imagine why they thought we'd be interested. Still, we appreciated the gesture.

The general had very kindly offered us his own room for the night, showing us to very basic quarters with two single beds in it. Just before he left us, he turned to me and handed me a long wooden stick. 'This is for the green mamba. It hasn't been in for a few nights, but if it does appear, just hit it with a stick and it'll leave.' The green mamba snake, we later learned, is highly venomous, but even without this knowledge, myself and Kim didn't sleep a wink that night. We returned to Liberia the following day to observe the rather chaotic handing-in of AK-47s and other weapons as part of the disarmament drive.

Then we went on to our next stop, Uganda. It was the most beautiful, lush place, so fertile and green, but wrecked by the civil war that had been rumbling on and on in the north of the country for the previous eighteen years.

Mind you, if you just visited Kampala, Uganda's capital, you'd never think there was a war on. At the time, we could see there was a growing middle class there, playing games like rugby and golf and spending evenings in one of the brand new cinemas or shopping malls that have sprung up in the city. Meanwhile, up north, the civil war raged on. Many of its soldiers were children, kidnapped from their families in the darkness of the night and press-ganged into Joseph Kony's notorious Lord's Resistance Army. I can still remember driving around the border town of Gulu, at the heart of the conflict, at night, watching the crowds of young children who flooded into town, sent by their parents from country villages to be out of reach of the LRA. Up to 20,000 children would sleep in night camps, singing hymns and telling stories before sleeping. It was so strange to look at them, innocently snoring away, while just down the road, in the GUSCO Centre for Child Soldiers, former child soldiers – many of them killers – were looked after and rehabilitated. I'll never forget the sight of a roomful of these children watching *The Sound of Music*, eyes wide at Julie Andrews singing, 'so long, farewell, auf wiedersehen, goodbye.' These same children had been forced to drink human blood and to kill other children as members of the LRA.

However, of all the countries I visited for *Far Away Up Close*, it was Bosnia that left the strongest mark on me. I think it's probably easy to dismiss faraway conflicts in Africa, but when they happen in twentieth-century Europe, and in a place that was once a package holiday destination, they're harder to ignore.

'In Bosnia, there are 400,000 professional killers,' the policeman told me as we stood in the hills overlooking the Bosnian city of Sarajevo. 'And 40,000 of them are in Sarajevo.' We filmed this episode of *Far Away Up Close* in July 2005, ten years after the end of the vicious civil war in the former Yugoslavia between the country's ethnic groups, the Serbs, Croats and Muslims. The city of Sarajevo was under siege for three and a half years – the longest siege of a country's capital in the history of modern warfare. During that time, it is estimated that almost five thousand civilians were killed by the Serbian troops that had encircled the city.

What astonished me was just how close the war still felt to so many people in Bosnia. The rest of the world had moved on, but here it didn't feel so long

since neighbour had been pitted against neighbour.
Javor was one of them, a man who took me through
the rolling summer countryside. He explained that at
the outbreak of war, he had been like everyone else
in Sarajevo, just getting on with his life. But the siege
forced him into the fighting, to defend the city: 'I had
friends who called me and said, "We should fight,
we should defend ourselves, or they will come down
and kill all of us. Should we wait to be executed like
sheep or will we do something?"' We were driving
along the road and he stopped talking to point out
an innocent-looking stretch of woodland, behind
which had lain the infamous Omerska concentration
camp. Here, Bosniaks and Croats were rounded up
as part of the Serbian programme of ethnic cleansing.
A clip of video that I watch later reminds me, as I see
emaciated men standing behind barbed wire, their
eyes dark, their cheeks hollow – echoes of a time
Europe hoped to never see again.

Muharem Mursalovic was one of them. Held
in Omerska for six months, enduring beatings and
deprivation, he was still living in the area when I
met him. He told me that he saw his former captors
every day. 'Some of them even try to say hello,' he

explained to me. 'They think that by ignoring all this, it will be forgotten.' His fear was that if the war was forgotten so quickly, it could very easily happen again.

When I went to Sarajevo, I met a journalist who has reported extensively on post-conflict Bosnia. Before the war, she struggled to tell the difference between Serb, Muslim and Croat. A Muslim herself, she had grown up in a devout family, but ethnic differences never bothered her, so much so that she didn't notice that she was attending school with the son of Radovan Karadžić. 'I didn't care,' she said bluntly, 'but today, I do care, especially when I meet people who are Serbs and who are aged like I am [sic] ... because I always wonder did they take part in a war, because I don't feel comfortable being friends with someone who had maybe shot at me during the war.' And the war criminals were still around, not just the leaders like Karadžić and Mladić (who have since been captured and convicted), but many others, many of them walking around the city. As my journalist friend said, 'You can't arrest half of the country and I feel that half of the country are war criminals.'

Our next trip was to the site of the worst massacre to take place since the Second World War – Srebrenica, a tiny mining town whose name is burned into the memory of anyone who remembers the Yugoslav War. On 8 July 1995, the Serbs attacked Srebrenica. Up to 30,000 people fled to the UN safe zone a few kilometres outside the town, but later that afternoon, Ratko Mladić and his Serb forces marched right in, reassuring everyone that they would be safe, but split the women and children from the men. The women and children left in a convoy of buses, but up to 8,000 men and boys were killed.

Since that terrible July day, a dedicated group of professionals and locals has been steadily excavating the mass graves that pockmark the countryside, to disinter and identify the bodies of the countless Bosnian Muslims killed here. I can still remember the mass burial site we saw in the most beautiful mountain meadow, filled with wildflowers and mint. They brought in a little digger, which took off the top layer of earth, and then moved in to carefully brush the earth away. The first body I saw was slightly mummified, but I was told he was in his early twenties. He was wearing a tweedy jacket. His legs and torso broke apart as he was removed from the grave, and further examination revealed that in his breast pocket he had a tube of Aquafresh toothpaste and a toothbrush. I wondered at this, and the idea that when he left his home that day, he thought he'd need to brush his teeth. The stench of rotting human flesh from the mass grave was overpowering, and all we could do was reach down and grab a few leaves of the wild mint that grew there and hold it under our noses to take the smell away.

One person involved in the opening of graves was a former teacher, Murat. His brother had disappeared during the war, and ever since he had devoted himself to the work of finding remains. Murat found a Russian pocket watch that had stopped at 6.22 p.m. In the eight years that he'd been working, he had found more than fifty mass graves. He prayed that Allah would help them in their work. 'My mother was waiting for three years,' he explained. 'Every morning, every evening, she was waiting at the door with the same question, "Have you heard anything about Kasim?" That was my brother. That's something that I'll never forget. It's in my head all the time.'

Visiting that grave was something we'd never forget either. It was only ten years since the war and the events seemed so recent, the bitterness still so strong. An older woman whose cottage was near the mass grave spat at us as she passed by. It was clear to us that the Serbs still living there didn't like the international community coming and uncovering their war crimes, because they, too, felt like victims in a way, hard though it may be to believe. Frankly, I found it hard not to hate the Serbs myself, particularly when I visited the International Commission on Missing Persons (ICMP) morgue in Tuzla, where they take care of the remains, carefully washing the mud away from the bones, trying to assemble as much of a person as they can, cataloguing and labelling, before carefully packing them away in white plastic bags. One lady showed me a photo of her son. She had come to the ICMP morgue to give a blood sample, hoping that her DNA would match one of the little piles of human remains. As the programme supervisor explained to me, reuniting people with their loved ones and ensuring a proper burial was an essential humanitarian task. For me, it was the little possessions that were the most poignant – the toothpaste, the pocket watch, pictures of family and friends. It was heartbreaking.

Making the *Far Away Up Close* documentaries was an education on so many levels. I was struck recently by the great reporter Fergal Keane revealing his PTSD following years of reporting on wars and atrocities. I was thankful not to have experienced that, even though so much of what I'd seen, both at home and abroad, disturbed and upset me. Unlike Keane or, say, Jeremy Bowen – a prominent news reporter on the ground during the Yugoslav War who went on to report from the Middle East – my foreign reporting marked one period in my life, not years and years of exposure to atrocity. I can only imagine what others go through when the horrors are multiplied over time. For some reporters, however, it's easy to get sucked into the foreign correspondent glamour, to say, 'Hey, look how far I can take it,' or, 'Look how close I can get to the gunman,' but for me, there's a fine line between ego and wanting to be the best that you can be. When you're travelling the world on licence fee-payers' money, your only goal is to get them the story. My only job in making this series was to bring the story home, to help in our understanding of a complex world.

The series took six weeks to film, a long trip, and not an easy one. I missed home and Conor desperately. Eventually, I got into Dublin airport late one rainy evening in September 2005, to find Conor waiting for me in the arrivals hall. 'You didn't need to come out at this hour,' I said to him, even though I was thrilled to see him. I was home.

The next morning, when we woke up, he said, 'Keelin, I didn't tell you last night, because you were so tired, but there's something wrong with your mother.' That was when I found out that my mother, Orna, had ovarian cancer. We were devastated. We couldn't imagine losing Mum at the age of sixty-one: it was simply too much to take in.

CHAPTER 6

COMING TO TERMS
LATE OCTOBER 2019

Winter is marching in. The last leaf has fallen from my lovely tree, darkness falls at six o'clock and the streets are shadowy and damp. It's my least favourite time of year, even if the air reverberates with the sounds of illegal bangers and firecrackers. The children are at school, Lucy in her first year in secondary school and Ben in fifth class in primary. Their busy lives go on while I sit here, in the slipstream. The house seems to be holding its breath: we all are, as we wait for news from America. Sometimes I feel that everyone is just waiting for me to die, but then I brighten. Maybe I won't, I think. Maybe I'll be like that woman whose stage 4 cancer was reversed and who is now happily kayaking around America, having the time of her life. Maybe.

Because I'm losing my hair, I wear one of my wigs when I'm out and about. As I mentioned before, I'm naturally dark and haven't gone grey so far – not that I'm boasting! – but the wig makes me look respectable, even if I find a scarf more comfortable: it makes my head itch less. I've opted for a synthetic wig, because real-hair ones alarm me slightly, and because you have to style them and look after them, far too much trouble for me. I've always found it interesting, though, to see the different styles of headdress in Oncology Day Care in St Vincent's. Some women wouldn't be seen without their wigs, others are wearing brightly patterned headscarves or neat little cancer hats, for want of a better word – a close-fitting cap that keeps the head warm. Some rock a completely bald head and they have my admiration, even if I wouldn't do so myself. It certainly makes a bold statement, but I wonder if it would be frightening for others. Maybe I'm basing this on my own experiences with Ben, who heartily disliked my bald head. Only a small child when I first had cancer in 2011, I think he associates it with fear and a lack of understanding of what was going on in his little life. I actually have a photo of me, bald, with Ben sitting on my knee and I feel a bit sad about that. He was obviously frightened by this new mother of his, so I try to be 'decent' for him now, wearing one of my headscarves when he appears.

⁓

Thinking of Mum's diagnosis and the utter shock of it makes me remember my own diagnosis when my cancer returned. It was 26 November 2016 and I was in St Vincent's the day after Janice told me the news. I'd come in to do a battery of tests to plan next steps, and I was utterly traumatised. I can still remember a poor phlebotomist coming in to get my blood sample at about six or seven o'clock the morning after I received the news from Janice. I was sobbing so much, I thought I'd be sick. The poor woman was trying to take my bloods, but I kept dissolving in tears. I wasn't handling it. Not one bit. Eventually, she had to give up, gently telling me that she'd come back. All I did then was stare out of my bedroom window at the golf course next to the hospital, at the golfers in their sweaters tapping balls into the holes on the green. I felt as if I was in another universe, on one side of a thick sheet of glass with my sickness, while on the other everything else was normal.

Janice, quite rightly, had been totally clear with me. When I asked her, 'How long have I got?', she said, 'The statistics say that most people will be dead within two years of this diagnosis.' As I write, it's been nearly three, but I know that I'm not special. I've been given an extra precious year with Conor and the children, but if these tests don't work, I'm still on my way out. It's as simple as that and I accept it. It took me a while, but I do. But I can't help feeling that everything about NIH – the National Institutes of Health – was written in the stars for me: I found out about it, I was American, they had a residents' place for Conor and me to stay in, the treatment was free. Surely now the stars would align again?

When I found out that I'd been accepted as a patient for tests in June this year, I was ecstatic. I hadn't been accepted for treatment, I must clarify;

just for tests to see if I was a suitable candidate. I had spent the previous weeks waiting and hoping, spending many a sleepless night wondering if it would happen. Suddenly, the future seemed to open up again, a future where I could be myself once more. It was all riding on this visit to the NIH in Washington, DC, so I'd done everything I could to look the part. I had even had a spray tan before I went over – imagine, a spray tan to get on a cancer trial! And I was too tired to shower it off, so it lasted me nearly the whole three weeks we were in America – good value for twenty euro. I had also bought a pair of mustard-coloured trousers in Dunnes. They were a bit lurid, but I wanted to be Little Miss Sunshine going in there, with a nice healthy glow. The reason for this was that they take patients' health into account when assessing them and I wanted to give them no reason to reject me.

In America, the tests began on Monday, a long battery of scans and other procedures. I had a dedicated nurse – and I wasn't even an in-patient at this point – along with a registrar who was doing his further study, and then a senior doctor. They were my team, visiting me often, giving me all the information I needed and passing on the results of the tests. The MRI was a nightmare because of my bone pain, but I didn't want to ask for too much Xanax in case they labelled me a drug user. It didn't fit with Little Miss Sunshine anyway! But the radiographers were very good about getting the cushions in the right places for support. Some people find scans frightening, but I just count along in my head to the *tack-tack* noises the machine makes to distract myself.

Finally, after about ten days in the US, they called us in for a meeting to tell us that we were 'on' for the next round of tests, more invasive procedures to harness my immune system. I was thrilled, even though it had been a rough enough ten days. I could have painkillers and steroids and anything I wanted, but I couldn't have cancer treatment, and now the strain was beginning to show.

They began the process by doing surgery on the lungs, removing pieces of cancer from the tissue, then they performed apheresis, which, in a nutshell, takes your blood and separates certain elements of it, returning the remainder to you. It resembles dialysis in a way and, in my case, involved sticking rods into my arms through which the blood was to drain. The lovely junior doctor came to see me the night before. A young guy, only about twenty-six or so, he cheerfully announced, 'Oh God, the apheresis is awful! I tried it myself – we have to try some of the things that we put our patients through – and that was just terrible.'

He made me laugh out loud. 'You've got this all wrong,' I told him. 'You're supposed to say, "It's not great, but you'll get through it," or something like that.'

He guffawed. 'Yeah, you're probably right.' And made no further attempts to reassure me. However, it was actually fine, a lot less uncomfortable than the MRI, and I knew that if I did the tests, I'd get closer to my goal of actually getting the treatment.

As a former scientist, I was interested in the process. What happens with the lung samples is that they take them to the lab and examine them to see how good you are at fighting your cancer. I don't think they found anything good about my ability to fight my cancer, so they were moving on to the next process, which was finding a way to nuclearise my cells to give them a weapon to fight the cancer. But to find a weapon, you need to find a target; and they were trying to find a target to engineer an immune cell from me to fight. And then they put the immune cells back into you. It all sounded very space-age, but I can remember the nurse saying to me, 'That bit is so disappointing. It just goes in via a little bag on a drip.' There would be no booming orchestral music, no cavalry coming down the hill, just a couple of hours of boredom and a drip. It's funny, I reported on various scientific discoveries during my working life, but I never imagined that I'd become a guinea pig in one of them. Cancer was something that other people experienced, not me. But tests are part and parcel of cancer treatment and I find that just getting on with them is the best option, as there isn't really an alternative.

$$\sim\!\!\varnothing\!\!\sim$$

Back in 2016, when Janice confirmed that the cancer had returned, and that it wasn't just in my bones, but in my bones and lungs and in multiple sites, I knew, without her having to tell me, that it was all over. I never thought it would return, but it had been lurking around me all along, in spite of regular scans and the best of supervision. I have no doubt that Janice wouldn't do anything differently: she could have scanned me every month and caused enormous anxiety to me and my family, not to mention costing the health system a fortune ... and to what end? I don't think about it like that in any way. I think Janice was an excellent oncologist and did her job brilliantly, and as soon as I was diagnosed, she got me on to the newest drug, Palbociclib. Janice had been involved in some of the clinical trials and this new form of chemotherapy was the great hope in treating breast cancer. That drug held my cancer at bay for a period of about nine months, but in retrospect, I regret that I didn't see it that way. I didn't think that being 'held' was a good thing: I wanted a miracle. A cure. And now, after two years, America is holding out that possibility. All I can do is hang on and wait and wonder what on earth could be keeping them. It's now October and it's been almost four months. Four months of being in limbo after all those tests. Surely they must know something by now, I think.

When I was told the bad news in 2016, Conor and I made the choice to tell the children that the cancer had returned, but not to let them know how serious it was. The medical team started me on radiotherapy virtually immediately because I was in a significant amount of bone pain, and one night I ended up taking the kids in with me because we were heading off to Funderland afterwards. Imagine! We must have been insane. That evening one of the machines was broken, so there was a backlog and after a while, the men who were there for prostate cancer treatment began to grumble. The women didn't fuss, but after an hour or two I was getting weary and uncomfortable perched on a hard chair. And then a woman whom I recognised as having worked with Conor in advertising many years ago came up to me and said, 'Keelin, I just saw you there. I'm next. You take my slot.' I nearly cried with gratitude at the sheer humanity of that. Of course, an old man gave out, but the lovely radiotherapist simply said to me, 'Leave him to us.'

So I had my blast of radiation and then we bundled the kids into the car to go to Funderland and none of us enjoyed it. It was early December, freezing and grim, and I didn't have the energy to go on a single thing. The kids and Conor had about five goes on a water slide and then we went home.

Made in the USA, 1968.

Courtesy Mary Shanley
Orna Shanley (mother)

The size of my head!

Playtime.
Indianapolis, 1969.

Assorted 'Loreto Girls': Kyla O'Kelly, me, Debbie Pearce and Nicola Byrne at Fiona McHugh's wedding, 2002.

With my best friend, Nicola Byrne, and some dodgy jeans. Barcelona, 1991.

On a weekend away in Paris in 1997. Little did I know that I'd be living here just a few years later.

Our wonderful wedding day.
Sligo, 29 January 2000.

Bosnia, 2006. Bringing out the dead, 10 years after the Srebrenica massacre. (*Courtesy of Animo TV*)

On patrol with the Irish Army in Liberia in 2006. (*Courtesy of Animo TV*)

Reporting from Malaysia for *No Frontiers* in 2002. (*Courtesy of Frontier Films*)

A moment of calm, 2009. (Lucy styled her own hair with a scissors!)

Ben trying on the wig I hoped I wouldn't need again, 2012.

Dad and June's wedding day. Dún Laoghaire, 2014. With Muireann, Eoin, Emma and Niamh.

Harold's Cross Park on Lucy's Holy Communion day, 2015.

Interviewing Bill Gates for *Morning Edition*. (© *RTÉ*)

The 'anchor dollies' – as Caitríona called us – hard at work! (© *RTÉ*)

I started on *Crimecall* in 2016. It was really then that people started recognising me in the street!

With the wonderful Eavan Boland at the Irish Book Awards in 2017.

Flying with the wind in Phoenix Park in 2015.

One of my favourite trees. Phoenix Park, 2016.

Waiting for news. Washington DC, June 2019.

Braving the 'Baltic' sea at Rosses Point, Co. Sligo. February 2019.

Cruising the Shannon at summer's end, 2019.

Relaxing with darling Dougal, August 2019.

Local fireworks with my loves, Halloween 2019. Wonder never dies.

None of us had the heart for it really, particularly poor Lucy; it was too much for her. I don't know if they knew I was dying at this point, but it was in their vocabulary and even though, being kids, they were desperate to go to Funderland, at the same time they couldn't cope with it. So we trudged home to our new house, purchased just months before my diagnosis, which was basically half-renovated and in complete chaos. We tripped over mountains of cables and bags of plaster to the kitchen and sat sadly down at the table for a makeshift dinner. Even Dougal was sad, resting his chin on his paws under the table.

At this point, believe it or not, we hadn't told anyone else that my cancer had returned. We just wanted to find out as much as we could before breaking the news to others, beginning, of course, with Dad. Until we'd told Dad, we'd told nobody. It was getting difficult, though, to explain my sudden disappearances. He might call to see how I was and be told I was off 'doing research' for a programme when in fact I was in hospital having tests. It was really tough, but we didn't want to worry him until we knew exactly what we were dealing with, and because I didn't want to see the look on his face when we did.

The other day, Dad said to me, 'I find it extraordinary that you managed to have such a big career when it was so interrupted by cancer.' I really don't think I'm any way special simply because I kept on working. I bumped into a nurse when going in for a scan one day and, after a little while, noticed that she was wearing a wig. So I wasn't alone. Thousands of women keep going because they want to, or have to. A lot of people said to me, 'Why don't you just give it up?' To which my answer would be 'Why, when I'm able to keep going?' I believe that it's possible to live a relatively normal life while having cancer treatment, and I really wanted to do that. I also feel that there is a choice when it comes to working while having treatment. I'm well aware that that's a controversial thing to say and people might not like it, but it was true for me. I had many advantages, admittedly, but there's something defeatist about the word 'cancer'. It is unlike any other word in illness. It comes with so much baggage: that you're going to die in pain, with no hair and it's just a miserable, awful disease – but this is no longer a certainty in cancer and I hope that the way I've lived through it is testament to that.

Caitríona Perry popped in to see me the other day with her gorgeous baby girl, Molly. She's on maternity leave and looks a great deal more relaxed than I did as a young mum. As we cooed and chattered at the baby, Caitríona reminded me of our mutual pact on the *Six One*. 'Do you not remember?' she said. 'You kept my secret and I kept yours.' Of course. When I was diagnosed for the second time, she was one of a select few in RTÉ who knew that I was living with cancer. I swore her to secrecy because I didn't want to be 'Keelin with cancer' but simply 'Keelin who reads the news' or 'Keelin who's got a nose for a story'. And so, as friends do, she covered for me when I was absent for treatment, helping out on some of my stories. And when she told me excitedly that she was expecting, but didn't want to share the secret just yet, I did the same for her. We were a great team.

A lot of people ask me if I really do feel as cheerful as I appear and I sometimes wonder about that. I'm not trying to kid myself, but while I'm still alive, and I can still love my family and friends, I have a lot to be cheerful about, strange as it may seem. My friend Katie Hannon came to visit me the other day and she said, 'Keelin, I'm going to write an explainer in this book, a little preface to the effect that you're not normal ...' and we both laughed. I think, deep down inside, I'm not blind to this tragedy, but once I accepted it there is nothing more I can do except make the biggest effort to stay healthy, to stay well, to spend time with my loved ones; I need to surrender to it. I don't want to lose the rest of the life I have to live by turning it into a grieving process. Everyone's going to grieve, but they can do it afterwards. They don't need to be doing it with me.

When Mum was dying, the soccer World Cup was on in Germany, and we'd all gather at home or in her room in hospital to watch matches and to be with her. We knew that she was dying, but at the same time it was lovely to spend the time with her. Plenty of people never get the chance to say goodbye to loved ones, so in a funny way, we were lucky to have had that opportunity. I used to bring her documentaries to watch in the Blackrock Clinic, which might sound strange – offering your ailing mother gritty documentaries – but I knew that Mum would still find them interesting. She had always been very socially conscious, and she'd drilled it into all five of her children that we were lucky and that life was very different for others. And, like all good mums, she'd tell me how great I was!

∽∾

One documentary I always associate with Mum is a film the team made on sex trafficking into Ireland. Memory is funny and things are never quite how you remember them – particularly now, when I have difficulty remembering what I did yesterday. Time distorts some things and renders others so clearly. Nonetheless, I don't think I'll ever forget what one woman said. 'These men, they come for me and I'm crying.' Coco was sitting in a dim little hotel room in Bucharest, telling us about being lined up in a Dublin hotel along with other prostitutes for Irish punters to choose their favourite. Even though tears were streaming down Coco's cheeks, one Irish man chose her. It's barely credible.

I think I also remember the documentary because of everything else that was going on in my life at the time. We were coming to terms with Mum's terminal illness and at the same time Conor and I were desperate to become parents. I had always known that I wanted to be a mum, but after six years of marriage there was no baby and I'd embarked on a course of IVF treatment, which would result in our precious Lucy. Everyone who has had IVF knows that it's a gruelling process, and even in Bucharest, I had to set the alarm to wake during the night to use one of the many medications I'd been given, but I was as determined to film this story that we'd been trying to access for so long as I was to become a mum, so I just went with it. In hindsight, I think I must have been mad, but I'm a bit of a terrier when it comes to a good story. I'll just keep on going until I've got it.

Sex trafficking is a hidden crime in Ireland, so we had to dig deep, which is how my colleagues and I ended up in a van in Thomas Street on a Saturday afternoon, watching as many as forty men go into a well-known brothel. They didn't have horns on their heads; they were just ordinary men in scruffy jackets and jeans, suits and sneakers, some young, some older. Our brilliant researcher, Paul Murphy, had done some digging and had been presented with a variety of excuses by the men visiting the place: young men would visit on their way into town for a

Saturday night so that they wouldn't feel the need to 'bother' women later. They'd get it all out of their system in advance, they told him, and just get on with having a night out with the lads. Unbelievable, really, but I've always been struck by what goes on in our own towns and cities, hidden in plain sight. I don't honestly think the punters saw the girls they were using as fully human, with their own lives and feelings. There seemed to be an attitude that paying for the service gave them the freedom to do what they wanted and they rationalised it by telling Paul, 'Well, she wouldn't be here if she didn't want to be.'

But what the punters ignored was the fact that many of the women in this brothel, like most brothels around the country, had been trafficked into Ireland by ruthless gangsters, treated like slaves and abused by Irish men. The legislation hadn't caught up with this uncomfortable truth, but we were determined to expose it and to get to the heart of where the girls were coming from at the time, which was Romania and Lithuania. Things are very different today, but back in 2006, Romania was about to join the EU (Lithuania had joined in 2004), so it was trying to present the best possible face to its European neighbours. At the same time, it was one of the poorest countries in the EU, and after twenty-four years of the Ceauşescu regime, it really had no infra-structure or wealth.

Anyway, back in January 2006, with less than one week to go to our departure for Bucharest, we had next to nothing. Janet, my brilliant producer/director, was rattled. She knew that I had to be back in Dublin by St Valentine's Day to go to the IVF clinic and she really wanted to look after me, as well as dealing with the fact that we had less than a week to make it all work. Documentary-making to a deadline is a stressful process at the best of times, but this was at a whole other level. The problem was, we were finding it hard to get trafficked women who were willing to speak to us. Finally, the International Organisation for Migration found two women who had been trafficked into Ireland and who were now in a safe house back in Romania. So we had our two living examples of the horrors of the process. But I had nothing else – no experts, no nothing. Still, I presented poor Janet with it and, quite rightly, she thought I was mad. We were close to getting two other women in Lithuania who had also been trafficked into Ireland to do interviews, but we still hadn't secured their permission to take part – when it came to women's testimony, safety in numbers was vital – not to mention that there was also a huge amount of planning involved in flying to multiple locations in two countries, which hadn't even been looked into, and with only a week to do this, it was a stressful time.

In spite of Janet's misgivings, we reached a compromise. I would go to Bucharest, and she would complete the Lithuanian leg of the trip. We booked our flights to Bucharest and off we went, with an outline of our wish list for our documentary, but nothing firm, apart from our two girls. Initially, we planned to 'buy' a woman in Romania: we knew from our sources that the going rate was €3,000. Needless to say, we were not going to actually traffic a woman – we simply wanted to show how easily it could be done and how cheap the lives of these often very young women were. I can still see us sitting in a car outside a brothel on an anonymous street in Bucharest. Cedric Culleton, our amazing cameraman, was to be our decoy; he would go in to 'buy' a woman with his mobile phone switched to record. I can't believe the risks we took. We wouldn't be allowed to do that now – there would be a full risk-assessment plan – but I think you need to go with your instincts as a journalist. You also need to think things through: why would a trafficker want to kill us, even if he knew we were journalists? We didn't pose any real kind of threat to them, and as far as they were concerned, the stakes weren't that high.

Once Cedric had set up the purchase, he was to go to a posh hotel in Bucharest to complete the transaction. The meeting was like something out of a movie. We'd followed the traffickers in their car to the hotel and we went in, pretending we didn't know Cedric, and sat down at an adjoining table. I think we did the mobile phone trick again to record the transaction. The brothel owner was joined by a casually dressed woman for the negotiations – she looked like somebody's mum. I was astonished at the time that a woman would involve herself in the trafficking of other women, but I was naive then. I understand now that it's all about money. I think in a developing democracy money is really, really important in a way that it isn't in a more developed country like Ireland. Where there is some safety net, you don't need to do utterly outrageous things for money, like travel overseas in a tiny inflatable boat with no lifejacket, having handed a people trafficker thousands for the privilege. I filmed documentaries all over the world, from Haiti to Honduras, and it was always the same: when money was in short supply, people would do anything to get hold of it.

At the hotel, Cedric negotiated the price for the girl with the duo and they showed Cedric her papers to prove that she was real. Then they asked Cedric a battery of questions about what his requirements were and what he liked. I think the arrangement with the men was for the girl to be handed over the following day in exchange for the cash, which Cedric had showed them. But they pursued us afterwards, calling Cedric and demanding, 'When are you coming for the girl? She's ready, she's ready.' I'd say at €3,000, she was the probably the priciest kind of woman you could buy in Romania. We were just rich Europeans in their eyes, and it was a seller's market. It was just so sad.

Our next encounter was to be even more of a shock. I knew that many things were still undeveloped in Romania, but nothing had prepared me for our visit to a Roma family in Bucharest. Trafficking was a huge problem in the Roma community and when we were presented with an opportunity to meet someone with real-life experience, we jumped at the chance. It was minus 25°C and sleeting as we made our way through a warren of narrow streets to what I can only describe as a shed. It had no windows, a mud floor and contained an entire family – Granny, Mum and Dad and two children, along with a horse. Frankly, it was a biblical scene – we were visiting a manger in twenty-first-century Europe. The story we were told made our hair stand on end. One of the girls told us that her sister's twin babies had been trafficked to Italy to be sold to an Italian couple. Now, I have heard many stories in my career, some harrowing, but this left me floored, unable to comprehend that such a thing could be happening so close to our cosy modern European comfort zone. But I suppose my sensitivities were heightened by the shining hope that soon I would have a baby of my own, if the IVF treatment worked out.

Today, Romania is one of the success stories of Europe, with economic growth booming. The pictures we probably all remember, of sad, empty-eyed children in dismal orphanages, have been replaced by images of shiny consumption and pretty cafés on the streets of Bucharest. Then, it was very different. Women and children were regularly trafficked to other European countries, including our own. And when they were there, they were treated appallingly, as our visit to a safe house demonstrated. The stories we heard there sent shivers down our spines. Coco, our main interviewee, had been told she was coming to Ireland to be a childminder in Cork and she flew in with her sister's boyfriend to discover an entirely different plan for her. We don't know for sure, but I reckoned her sister knew. Imagine, betrayed by your own sister. It shows the lengths people will go to to get ahead, or maybe just stay afloat.

Meeting Coco presented me with a dilemma: not just how to convey the horrors of her experience to Irish viewers, but also how to break through the shield she had built around herself since she'd gone to the safe house. Coco had had a great deal of therapy, quite rightly, but initially every question I asked her was met with a bland response, the kind of therapy-speak familiar to watchers of American TV dramas, and I felt that I had to just keep pushing her until I got the frank answers I felt the viewers needed. This might seem ruthless, heartless even, but as a journalist, my responsibility is always to the viewer. I always think, what does the person at home want to know? It can be difficult to get viewers really involved in what can often seem like distant problems, and I have learned that the best way is simply to elicit the unvarnished truth from the interviewee. That doesn't mean that the encounter is easy – in fact, interviewing Coco was one of the toughest jobs I've ever done, both emotionally and professionally.

It also has to be said that, sometimes, the tougher the experience, the better TV it will make. This might sound cynical, but I know from experience that sometimes only the most striking images will connect with viewers. A lot has changed since 2006 and we've certainly grown more accustomed to seeing shocking pictures, but to me, the memories of interviewing Coco and visiting that Romanian prison have never faded. We were brought into a room, about thirty feet square, in which bunks were piled high to the ceiling, pushed right up against each other, covered in gaudy blankets and worn sheets. I'd say there were at least fifty beds in the room. The traffickers were young, good-looking Albanians – truly scary men – and the way they worked was to recruit a 'girlfriend' locally, then suggest they just do one thing for them to prove their devotion. The next thing, the girls were being beaten and used in sex work. I can still remember one man explaining his actions to me, chillingly: 'Did they expect we'd treat them like princesses?'

After coming out of that prison, I was shell-shocked. The conditions were so Dickensian, I felt I had to tell someone what I'd seen, so I rang Dad. Poor Dad had just come from the hospice, where he had been planning Mum's final days, but being Dad, he put a brave face on things, pretending that he was only delighted to hear from his traumatised daughter. He told me that Mum was fine, that they were just getting a bed ready, 'in case', but I *knew*. It's an irony that I'm making the same arrangements now myself. I've even done some charity work with the hospice and now here I am, ready to book my bed in the same place where my mother died.

At that moment, in the van, it all came together: that was really the first time the imminence of Mum's death hit me, the struggle for a baby, that awful prison ... It all came at me like a tidal wave, and it was completely overwhelming. I flew home that afternoon, leaving the others behind to get what we call GVs – general views – such as street scenes to fill out the core content of the documentary. Now it was time to focus on the IVF, I told myself. I had made my documentary, and it had been harrowing, but I was ready to go, to begin a new life.

Unfortunately, my body didn't agree with me. In spite of all our best efforts, after a number of days there were no eggs. I couldn't believe it. And when I was told that simply taking a day off could help, I was even more doubtful. I didn't believe that working hard would have anything to do with what my body was doing, but I was wrong: I took my day off and, suddenly, zero eggs became twenty. It was an eye-opener! It's a funny thing that with all the benefits of modern society, we don't realise how primeval our bodies are – it's not necessarily a welcome thought, but I knew now that I'd have to compromise if I wanted a baby.

We were so lucky. On St Valentine's Day 2006, our precious Lucy Valentina came into being; made of the two of us, just with a bit of extra science thrown in. I am conscious that, as I write this, she will be mortified, but I want her to know how desperately she was wanted and how much we love her.

The documentary went out in May 2006 and my mother died in June of that year. As a family, we were devastated, but we had stopped fighting the idea of her death some time before, even though it seemed so unfair. She was only sixty-one years of age – far too young to die, robbed of the pleasure of meeting the grandchildren, apart from my sister Muircann's daughter, Amy. She would have loved having them all running around. Dad was bereft without her: he'd lost his other half, the woman who had supported him in everything he did, while holding down her own job as a physiotherapist and raising five children. The only consolation we had was that we'd had that precious time with her. And that it had ended the way she and Dad had wanted it, at home, surrounded by us all.

The programme caused quite a stir, I remember. Back then, the whole team watched it together in

RTÉ because we had put so much into it – we'd given it our all. We would end up winning an IFTA for it and never had any award felt more hard won. Now, as I watch the images and recall the stories, I remember that Mum had watched the documentary sitting up in her bed in hospital and that I wished I'd gone up to watch it with her. She was always so proud of me. She kept all my clippings from the newspapers, which I still have, and always rang me after every programme, declaring, 'Oh, Keelin, that was brilliant,' no matter what the subject or format. So I had wished we had watched it together. But it was only one tiny regret. That was the great thing about our family. We'd come together, we'd minded Mum as well as we possibly could, and when she died, none of us felt we should have done things any differently.

∽

Mum always used to say that it's amazing what you can get used to, and it is. I was devastated when I was diagnosed in 2016 and while I wait for news from the States, I realise that I have become used to my new life. Being pushed around Dún Laoghaire in a wheelchair has become the new normal, just as I used to push Mum around Monkstown in her wheelchair fourteen years ago. I can clearly remember her saying to me that she had no regrets. Neither do I. I don't wish I'd done anything differently with my life. I don't have a 'bucket list'. I don't want to travel the world, or climb Everest, or even read the news one last time – although I do feel a touch of envy at missing Election 2020, the first that I won't have covered in all my time as a journalist. All I want is to be here, now, with my family and friends, for as long as possible. I just want a bit more time. If the news from America is good, I'll have it.

In the meantime, I'm going to live every day as best I can and I'm going to hope. Hope is a wonderful thing. It makes me feel that I'm not just ploughing forward to my grave. There is a chance and even though I know, deep down, that it's a ghost of a chance, it's a chance all the same.

CHAPTER 7

LOST IN TRANSITION
NOVEMBER 2019

I can really only shuffle these days, between bed and bathroom. It's a maddening side effect of the steroids I now take every day: they weaken the leg muscles terribly. Two milligrams of dexamethasone, along with a cocktail of other little pills to help with the toxic effects of the chemo: anti-nausea tablets, painkillers, temazepam for pain, co-trimoxazole and zopiclone, as well as Xanax. I used to be afraid of taking a headache tablet, but now, I think, 'Bring it on!' I often treat myself to a Xanax in the evening to help with the long nights. Pain always seems worse at three o'clock in the morning and the last thing I want these days is to lie awake, contemplating my existence.

I tell myself that I don't mind the lack of mobility, but I find it hugely frustrating – I so desperately want to move freely, but I just can't. Instead, I have to rely on my ever-patient family to lift me in and out of my wheelchair and to take me into Dún Laoghaire for a little jaunt to the shops. I have to admit, I have had a soft spot for Shaws ('Almost nationwide!') since we moved back here, and these days the most exciting thing on my agenda is a trip to their bedding department. I love the crisp feeling of their sheets and the fluffiness of their towels. If I'm feeling particularly spontaneous we might venture to Debenham's in Blackrock. The kids are a bit cavalier about these trips, abandoning me in the jumper section and wandering off to look at more interesting things. I can't say I blame them and I'm thankful that they don't feel they have to hover around me.

I'm also trying to ignore a new rattling sound in my chest. I've had a niggling cough for a while now, and my chest heaves with the effort of breathing.

When I first started rattling, I lay awake for a night in bed, listening to it, knowing that it wasn't 'the end' but wondering all the same. What would it be like when it came for me? Would I slip into a blissful coma, thanks to the opiates? Would there be pain, discomfort, confusion? Would my family suffer seeing me go like this? But then I remember my mother and how much time I spent with her as she succumbed to the slow process of dying. I was expecting Lucy at the time, and I'd go up to her bedroom in my family home in Monkstown and we'd admire the latest scan, Mum cooing over the blurry outline of an ultrasound picture. I feel lucky, in a way, to have this precious time with my family, perverse as it may sound.

Back in 2006, I knew that my days as an intrepid reporter might well change into something else. What I was doing came with a price: I wasn't easy for Conor to live with because of the pressures of the job, with constant travelling and deadlines; and really, I think the kind of in-depth reporting that I was doing can't be done for ever. It's too hard: there are only so many people in distress that you can meet before you either become cynical or get burnout, and there are only so many situations you can put yourself in before you end up getting tired. I still loved my work, but my children were, and are, the centre of my life. I was to take one last trip when the children were small, to Haiti, to film the aftermath of the disastrous earthquake in that country in 2010. But by that time, I was a mother of two and life would never be the same again.

I can still remember driving to the hospital on St Valentine's Day, 2006, to see if the IVF had been successful. I was a bundle of nerves. Lucy had been so wanted, and for so long, that it was almost too much to find out whether or not the latest attempt had been successful. The traffic, which had been slow all the way through the city, ground to a complete halt as we headed down Clanbrassil Street towards the river. I was driving, and the radio was on, then Conor's phone started to ring. He answered it and a voice called out 'Daddy?' into the silence. 'Hello?' Conor replied, but the phone went dead. It must have been an omen of sorts, because an hour later I had my scan and found out that I was pregnant with Lucy. It was a miracle, I knew. I felt like the luckiest woman in the world.

I worked throughout my pregnancy, as many women do, so I don't feel I deserve a medal, but I knew that life would change after Lucy arrived, so I was determined to make the most of things. I can remember taking my last pre-baby holiday with Conor to the New Forest in Hampshire, which was absolutely stunning, a vast space filled with all kinds of wildlife. We were staying in a little leaf-fringed cottage and it was pretty idyllic. Conor had stopped referring to Lucy's imminent arrival as 'The Emergency' and was getting more used to the idea of fatherhood, but he thought we should take a trip to make the most of our dwindling freedom. People tell you that your life will change utterly when you have children, but still, I think everyone has to experience it for themselves.

Conor was a keen DJ; he had a residency at the 'Strictly Handbag' club night for years, and had played at the Big Chill festival in the UK. We were tootling around Gloucestershire one morning when he got a call from an old friend in Italy, whose sister worked for the Fendi fashion label. They were wondering whether he might be free to DJ at a party in Rome for Madonna two days later. Conor was ecstatic and I knew that, break or no break, he just couldn't turn it down – nobody says no to the Queen of Pop!

We were both flown to Rome, where a driver picked us up and dropped us to our hotel, then it was up into the hills of Rome to a villa belonging to Silvia Fendi to check out the DJ set-up. It was gorgeous. We wandered from room to room, each with a drinks bar planted in the corner. I joked to the woman showing us round, 'Is there no TV?' and she said, 'Oh, this is just the party house. The villa is next door.'

That night we arrived for the party, which was actually in the villa's exquisite gardens. The place was filled with beautiful Italians and almost as many staff as guests. The trees were lit up with thousands of fairy lights and there was a full moon. It was magical, but at seven months pregnant – still just about able to travel, but only just – I was exhausted, so I left Conor to it before Madonna had even arrived. He was happy playing his set to this utterly fabulous audience, among them fashion designers Dolce & Gabbana and members of the Italian football team. Conor had a blast and I knew that it had been worth it. And then, a week after we returned, a parcel arrived containing a fabulous Fendi handbag – patent black leather with cool orange stitching – and a note from Silvia Fendi apologising for not making me feel welcome enough. I have never, ever possessed a designer handbag, so I treasured it; all the more because I knew that I'd soon be moving on to nappy bags.

When Lucy was born, on 24 October 2006, I really did regret that my mother wasn't alive so that I could thank her and understand more about how she had loved us so much. Motherhood seemed like such a miracle and I wondered, looking at my gorgeous baby girl, if she'd felt the same way, as if the Messiah had landed! I don't believe in the hereafter, but I like to think that Mum was somewhere out there, looking down on me, because all of a sudden all these nursery rhymes that she must have sung to me came into my head. I didn't even know I knew them, but there they were, 'Hush Little Baby, Don't Say a Word', 'Rock-a-Bye Baby'. I stared at Lucy for the whole night, unable to believe that she was now here, with me and Conor, and that she was utterly perfect. The hospital buzzed around me, but I was oblivious, so fixated was I on my precious baby.

But I was also nervous, afraid that every little hiccup was a sign of something serious. On our return home from the Coombe with Lucy in her little car seat, she began to be sick and I insisted that we turn around and head back to the hospital. They gently explained to me that it was probably just wind! I felt a bit of a fool. I also felt that I didn't have a role model now that Mum was gone, somebody to reassure me, to tell me that I was doing as well as I could, to give me advice which I'd then tell her was nonsense.

I'll freely admit that I went slightly crackers: every cough was pneumonia, every burp a sign of acid reflux. Like the time I rushed up to Crumlin Children's Hospital with Lucy one morning at four a.m. Her cheeks were red, she was dribbling and roaring, clearly in pain. 'She's not right,' I insisted to the doctor. 'What's wrong with her?'

The doctor, a nice young woman, examined Lucy carefully before replying, 'Maybe she's teething?' I was mortified. I had attended a hospital in the middle of the night because my baby was teething. In my defence, I had two cousins who'd died of cot deaths in infancy, so it was in my head that such a thing could happen.

They say that among the predictors of postnatal depression are bereavement and an IVF or assisted-conception baby. I didn't have postnatal depression but that first month with Lucy was challenging, to say the least. I think I was simply being a first-time mum who missed her own mum. Thankfully, I had Conor, who was a rock – unexpectedly, because by his own admission he had never considered himself a 'baby person' up to that point – but once he returned to work, I was on my own, just me and Lucy. I became the fittest woman in the city! Lucy just wouldn't take a nap unless she was moving: there was never any laying her in her cot for a couple of hours' peace. No matter how much I tried to tire her out, she still needed to be taken out in the buggy twice a day if there was any sleeping to be done. But I loved pushing her around our Portobello neighbourhood. We'd go to Harold's Cross Park, to the playground; or the lovely Iveagh Gardens, which was our secret place, to admire the dogs being walked or to amble through the maze in the rose garden when summer came; or St Stephen's Green to feed the ducks ... One morning we arrived so early that we had to wait at the gates for the groundskeeper to come and let us in because Lucy was such an early riser.

It was a strange and wonderful world, the two of us and our buggy, a little island of our own. I'd spent the previous decade often working seven days a week – work was my *raison d'être* – and I was really enjoying the change and the sense that motherhood meant that it was all no longer about me. There was a great freedom to that. I had also done a lot of homework on breastfeeding and I was determined to give it my best. It was tough going at first, but I got the hang of it and then I could enjoy being out and about without bottles or sterilising kits. In some ways, it reminds me of where I am now, an island, isolated by my illness; but again, there is a certain freedom in that, believe it or not. Last week a friend who had also had breast cancer came over and we reminisced about how minded we'd both felt in hospital. We literally had nothing to do except wait for dinner or for the nurse to drop by: it was like being a child again, at home in bed with the measles or the flu, bottle of Lucozade beside us. Being a mum was similar in the sense that our invisibility meant that we could just do our own thing, free from the responsibilities of life. The only thing I wished was that I'd known this sooner!

When Ben came along, twenty-three months later, on 22 September 2008, he came from nowhere. There was no IVF – he was just the loveliest surprise. (Although I found out that I was pregnant just days before Conor and I were headed to New York on a free trip that he had won for an advertising campaign. It was supposed to be a weekend of reviving the late-night fun of our child-free days, given that Lucy was staying at home. But it didn't work out quite like that: Manhattan may be the city that never sleeps, but I was barely up past midnight.)

Ben's babyhood was a lot less fraught than Lucy's. Of course, I mashed organic veg and meat for them both, puréeing it carefully for their little dinners, in spite of Conor insisting that they preferred the shop-bought stuff. But I didn't fret so much with Ben. I could just enjoy him, knowing that every little sniffle wasn't life or death. He was a real golden boy – white hair, big blue eyes, a gorgeous smile. And, of course, I think that no children are quite as special as my own. Obviously I am biased. It's a characteristic I inherited from my mother, who until her dying day protested that her beautiful baby son Eoin – now in his forties – was robbed of the title in the 1975 Tinahely Bonny Baby Competition. 'It was a fix!' she would proclaim.

I look at my children's every achievement and marvel at how terrific they are. Lucy with her stories and her creativity, Ben with his gung-ho energy and fascination about how the world works, which has been channelled so well in our new home. He follows the news and can probably identify more Irish politicians by name than Conor. He likes going sailing on Saturday mornings, returning wind-burned and happy, responding to my every question with a cheery 'I dunno'. And the two of them are very close, just like my brother Eoin and I were, in spite of trying to knock lumps out of each other.

Family has been one of the great joys of my life. Everyone says that, of course, but to me, I wouldn't change a single thing about the kids (or Conor!). My friend Judy Kelly, who is married to Eddie Doyle, said it to me once. 'You never try to *fix* your children, Keelin. You wouldn't change a hair on their heads, and that's lovely to see.'

Now I was a mum with two small children of my own *and* a full-time job. Every mum who has returned to work after having a baby will, I'm sure, relate to the exhaustion I felt. But at the same time, I was glad to have my own world to live in, to still be the person I always had been, even if I was wrung out at the end of every shift. I loved my life as a documentary reporter, but it was not a nine-to-five job by any stretch of the imagination, and even though Conor was brilliant at holding down the fort, he was busy too – and Ben was still being breastfed. He refused to drink bottles and would patiently wait for my return before spending the rest of the night feeding. I was managing, but it all felt like a bit of a merry-go-round in spite of our wonderful nanny, Nati. Everyone should have a Nati in their lives, I think! We discovered her through a good friend, Jenny McCrohan, who was looking to share the care of her daughter with another family, and so Nati came into our lives. She became an essential part of our family for five years. Married to Irishman Jim, she was the kindest person, a fantastic cook of Filipino food, which the children lapped up, and possessed of endless patience. We couldn't have got through those years without her.

That's not to say that I didn't experience my fair share of guilt, though. In my darker moments, I'd get angry with myself for having brought two children into the world and then saying, 'I'm off to look for drug dealers. I'll come back when you're sixteen.' Of course, it wasn't always like that, and as the years went on, it got easier.

Ken O'Shea was my boss at the time and he called me into his office and asked me if I'd go to Haiti to report on the aftermath of the January 2010 earthquake there. My first thought was absolutely not, but then I rationalised it. It was, after all, only ten days, and it might get Ben off the breast and onto the bottle! I didn't take it lightly, but my old sense of adventure kicked in – and I'd seen coverage of the earthquake myself and knew how catastrophic it had been. The offer to see things for myself was too tempting to refuse. I said I'd go, leaving Conor in charge on his own for ten whole days and Ben with a supply of bottles.

David Doran was my producer on the report – he's now a senior producer in RTÉ – and he hadn't yet been to a place like Haiti, where sanitation was an issue. And now, six weeks after the earthquake, the situation was even more dire than usual. I warned him, 'David, do not put your hands anywhere near your mouth.' I had spent a lot of time in Africa, and even though I'm a thumbsucker, I know that there are certain no-nos when you're travelling: you can't have your fingers near your face, you can't use tap water and you keep your mouth firmly closed in the shower. However, all my hard-won lessons couldn't have prepared me for what I saw in Port-au-Prince. A full month and a half after the earthquake, the place was still in chaos, piles of rubble and destroyed buildings, refugees stranded in makeshift tents while the jeeps of the many NGOs whizzed around the city. There were no fewer than seven hundred NGOs in Haiti after the earthquake, but it was hard to see what difference this had made to local people. All that seemed to be happening was a giant traffic jam, with the only practical things being done by the Haitian and US armies. The situation wasn't helped by the fact that the prisons had been destroyed, releasing four thousand criminals onto the streets – and that wealthy local landowners wouldn't donate land for rebuilding.

It was certainly the case that much of the country's infrastructure was destroyed in the earthquake – schools, government buildings, even the airport – which made it so much harder for Haiti's government to respond, but it also came back to the same story: inequality. We went up to the hills above the city to visit a local businessman and were greeted by servants, dressed in white, who opened the gates to let us in. The hum of air conditioning provided a cool backdrop to the expensive décor as this man sat on a pricey-looking sofa and told us why, exactly, he wouldn't give some of his land – which was vacant and not particularly valuable – to help in the rebuilding project. 'If they want my land, they'll have to compensate me.' This from a man whose own staff had been affected while he'd been untouched. It was hard to keep my objective journalist's hat on in the face of this indifference. I wondered if he'd ever been down in the bowels of the city to see things for himself – I doubt it.

However, I also knew that in order to bring things home to Irish viewers thousands of miles away, we would need personal stories, so we'd leave our hotel every morning, after our breakfast of chips

– the only food available, and very nice – in search of them. Our driver, a local man, knew where to go. At one point, we were driving along and I saw a JCB digging out the rubble of what looked like a school. I got out of the car to have a closer look. I thought we'd get a few shots, but then I realised that with every third bucket, there was a dreadful stench. It was unmistakeably that of a body, and a *child's* body, because this was a school. Six weeks after the earthquake, they were still digging bodies out of the rubble. What struck me as I watched in horror is that they may very well have been the children of the men and women walking up and down the road. Worse, bodies and rubble were simply piled into the back of a truck. They weren't even separating them out. It was all going into landfill outside Port-au-Prince – everything, including human remains. I don't blame the Haitians for that: the death toll was monumental – estimates at the time suggested between 200,000 and 300,000 – so to give every person a burial was just impossible. Body retrieval was big business, with local men hiring themselves out to scrabble around the ruins of collapsed buildings for the remains of people's families.

With the rainy season due any day, another huge problem was the fragility of the temporary housing. With so many homes destroyed or damaged (105,000 homes were destroyed and a further 208,000 damaged in the earthquake, according to the World Health Organization), some people had managed to build shacks out of corrugated iron, but many were just lines of rope with tarpaulins thrown over them and they wouldn't stand a chance once the rain started. We decided that we wanted to get a better idea of what life was like at night in Port-au-Prince, something nobody else was doing, so off we went. The first person we met was a young mum with her newborn in a tiny tent, and while we were talking, a tropical storm erupted all around us. The tent promptly collapsed and buckets of rain poured in as people frantically tried to hold it up. That poor woman. It was like the third circle of hell. I can still remember doing my piece to camera as the deluge came down around me.

Next, we went to a place called Cité Soleil, an area in Port-au-Prince that had the worst reputation of anywhere in the whole of Haiti. The area ended at the sea and local gangsters would rob ships as they passed. It was all gangs and guns, extremely dangerous, so we needed an escort from the Haitian armed police, who reluctantly accompanied us in four armoured jeeps. There, I saw people living under actual bedsheets, with no waterproofing, nothing. I couldn't believe it. As I was coming out of one of the dwellings, I said, 'My God, they've really suffered, haven't they?' A local man who lived there replied, 'Oh, we weren't touched by the earthquake; we've always lived like this.' That came as the biggest shock to me, that people could be living like this in the twenty-first century and that they had no other choices. In fact, one of the many prison breakouts involved people from the area, who made their way straight back to Cité Soleil.

We weren't in any danger – I don't think. As a journalist, I'll admit that we can sometimes be naive, thinking, Oh, they're not going to hurt me, but I suppose I was lucky that it never happened to me. People in Cité Soleil were as polite as could be, even though their trust in the system had completely broken down. I'm not sure if they were fine because of the armed guards, but I just had to have faith that they wouldn't attack a journalist: there was no reason for them to do so, even if the bullet-marked walls made me wonder ...

Rural areas weren't any better. Thousands of rural Haitian houses had been damaged or destroyed. To see for ourselves, we went out into the mountains as well, and it was clear that those people had been totally forgotten about because they'd had more food around them to eat, even if many crops had been destroyed; but water and supplies, all those kind of things, were not great at the beginning and they were significantly worse at the end. The earthquake was followed by a cholera outbreak that killed thousands. Then, in 2012, Hurricane Sandy cut a swathe through the country. Haiti has rarely seen good fortune, from the dictatorship of Papa Doc Duvalier that robbed the country of so much to the outbreaks of illness and natural disasters, not to mention reports of alleged widespread sexual exploitation committed by UN soldiers on local women and girls.

But it's not all bad news. The UN made a concerted effort to address cholera and has reduced the outbreaks by 90 per cent since that dreadful time, and politicians like Bill Clinton have tried very hard to build Haiti up, bringing a lot of textile factories to the island. Denis O'Brien's Digicel mobile phone company was also quick to get involved, setting up a Haiti Relief Fund after the earthquake hit. We were offered the use of one of the company's helicopters while we were there, but I thought it best to make our own arrangements. When you work in RTÉ, you have to be wary of anything that might potentially affect your objectivity. While I was there, I saw a lot of textiles, like school sweatshirts, headed for Ireland, and these factories provided a glimmer of hope for local people. They weren't run by Haitians, though, but by Chinese, because they had the expertise. But it was a start.

While I was going into the dangerous corners of Port-au-Prince, Conor was holding down the fort at home and managing just fine without me. The first night Ben woke up screaming, but after that he was happy, even adjusting to the bottle. I know that Conor worried about me, though. I've been to plenty of lawless places, but Haiti was unique in the sheer scale of the destruction and in the time it was taking to help people dig themselves out of the catastrophe. I was glad I'd seen it for myself, even though I'm unlikely ever to forget it. What really struck me was that once we crossed the border into the Dominican Republic, which shares the island with Haiti, it could not have been more different, at least on the surface. We'd been living on chips for ten days and now we sat down to lobster at a lovely seaside restaurant. It felt, frankly, quite bizarre and guilt-inducing after everything we'd seen.

When I returned from that trip, I hugged the kids as hard as I could, in spite of their protests. I was so, so lucky, I thought, to live in this lovely, safe country with my family. Never to have to face famine or war or natural disasters, even if I think we could do more to address our own problems in this country. We have everything compared to a country like Haiti, and I've often wondered why we don't try harder to fix things like the housing crisis. Could it be because there is a limit to how much we really care?

The trip to Haiti marked the end of an era for me. I knew that there wouldn't be any more assignments like that; it was time for change. I would miss the buzz of travel, but I knew the time was right to focus on things closer to home. Presenting might not be as hair-raising as foreign trips – although sometimes it could be! – but it fitted better with my home life, so the next few years were filled with *The Consumer Show*, election specials, *Morning Ireland* and filling in on the Sean O'Rourke show, all of which were fantastic. They were all live, current affairs programmes and they suited me down to the ground, because while it was intense, when it was over it was over, leaving me free to do the school run and to be home for dinner in the evening. Then came *Morning Edition* and a whole new phase in my working life.

Looking back at those years now, it seems that they passed in a blur of work, home and school, but I loved every minute of them. Recovering from my first bout of cancer gave me a new lease of life and a desire to make the most of it all. They say that having cancer forces you to live in the moment, and I suppose it does, but actually, it made me think about what I really wanted in life. Work was, and is, important to me, but being a parent mattered more. It still does, which is why I find it so hard to know how best to tell the children about what the future might hold. They know that the word 'death' is hovering in the wings, but until we get news from America, we're in limbo. We can't give them the certainty we'd like to give them, so we just wait.

CHAPTER 8

BEGINNINGS AND ENDINGS
NOVEMBER 2019

Resilience, they tell me, comes from being able to adapt to change. In fact, when I looked up the word in the dictionary, it refers to 'springing back into shape', to elasticity. Life has certainly taught me to be elastic, but there's no 'right' way to respond to life's challenges. Everyone copes with them in their own way. Perhaps I brushed them aside, always looking to the future, but that's no bad thing when it comes to dealing with cancer. It doesn't mean that I didn't take it seriously or that I minimised its effects on me and my family, but the simple act of keeping going worked for me. I'm not a fan of motivational quotes, but I firmly believe that keeping plodding along is the only thing any of us can really do.

A few days after I returned from the States in July, I headed in to St Vincent's for a check-up. Up to this point, I had been driving myself in, parking and heading upstairs in the lift without a bother. But now I suddenly found myself wondering if I had the strength to make it. Luckily, I had my stick with me, so I got into the lift, but between floors minus one and one, I began to sink groundwards, hanging onto the stick. I kept telling myself that I'd get up any minute now, but just couldn't.

A lady who was in the lift with me said, 'Can I help you?'

'Oh, I'm fine,' I said, hanging onto the stick for dear life! She kindly helped me into the ward and they just put me into a bed immediately. I didn't protest. Going to Washington had taken every ounce of strength I possessed and I was just worn out. As I lay there, I wondered if it had all been too much for my ailing body, but then I told myself that if I completed the treatment at NIH, it would all have been worth it.

It was a really bleak time, but it was during this period that I began to turn the idea of a book over in my mind. Niamh had first suggested it to me. We've known each other for so many years and she'd thought, quite wisely, I need to keep that girl alive and she needs a project. She was right: I didn't know when I'd get the call to go back to America and I desperately needed something to occupy my mind in the meantime. So I began to make notes from my hospital bed, jotting down little ideas, memories, recollections: some from childhood, some work escapades, some from the first time I was diagnosed, way back in 2011. It seems like a lifetime ago now. When Niamh brought in some material from the archives for me to look back on, to remember my younger self, I thought it might be depressing to see myself like that, full of vigour, but in fact, it's not: I find myself giving myself a little mental pat on the back. I did okay, I think. I wasn't bad.

The penultimate chapter of my work journey began in 2013, and it would be full of new and exciting challenges. Kevin Bakhurst was MD of

News at RTÉ at the time and he approached me about a new concept he was considering. *Morning Edition* was to be a two-hour morning magazine programme, running Monday to Friday, to be filled with news stories. It was, I suppose, a more serious alternative to the lighter breakfast fare on other channels. The newshound in me was terribly excited about the idea and I accepted the challenge. And it sure was a challenge! Filling a whole two hours every weekday morning is no joke. If you consider that *Newsnight* on BBC2 runs for a mere forty-five minutes, and longer breakfast shows have lifestyle features as well as news, two hours was a big ask. It was done on a total shoestring and we had a tiny team. Anthony Murnane was the producer and the nicest man to work with, but boy did we have our work cut out for us. Apart from Anthony, I was the presenter, Aisling Riordan was a reporter-researcher and Sally Anne Godson was researcher on it for a while, as were Kate Egan and John O'Driscoll. I truly felt as if I was in the Wild West of broadcasting, exploring brand new terrain.

Our ideas came from anywhere and everywhere. We would have a planning meeting at the end of each show for the following day, but quite honestly, we were so wrecked from being live on air for two hours that it wasn't all it might have been. We'd start early – very early! I would get up at five-thirty in the morning and sometimes I'd tiptoe downstairs and make porridge to eat in the car. At other times, Ben and Lucy would creep out of bed to join me in the kitchen for toast and a chat, which set me up for the day. Then I'd come in and head quietly to my desk before anyone saw me. I'd go through the running order for the show and make my own notes on my precious piece of A4, with the name of each of my interviewees on it and some sample questions, along with hints and tips. 'After item X, it's Y'; 'Keep an eye out for X', and so on. This piece of paper was vital; because things were changing so fast, quite often I'd see someone walking into studio and think, Who on earth is this and what are they here for? We were covering everything from bringing jobs to Ireland during the recession, to the fodder crisis of 2013, to life in Wheatfield Prison, then we'd segue to Jeffrey Archer's new novel. I was truly kept on my toes.

We interviewed a lot of authors and, of course, I'd have to have read their books, so I'd have my own notes on that. I got quite good at speed reading. And because we'd begin the show with a paper review, I'd listen closely to the reviews on *Morning Ireland* before eight o'clock, as well as looking at the papers myself, so that I could help my two guests select stories. Every morning, we'd invite two journalists to review the papers, like on Sky News and BBC News 24. That was my favourite part of the programme, because we used a lot of very young journalists. It was brilliant to have new voices, as well as to achieve ambitions like upping the numbers of female and younger guests. Also, we were ahead of the curve in terms of featuring a wide range of guests of different nationalities. Needless to say, things would often go wrong; people's mics would fall off and you'd have to pick them up from under the table, guests would say unexpected things and you'd have to ad lib furiously while wondering how to get out of controversy and so on. It was non-stop excitement.

Bill Gates was our first guest. I was ecstatic at this big coup but didn't make the most of it, I have to say. Sometimes when you get a big name, there are simply so many places to go with your interview that focus can be an issue. And you can pick the wrong subject. Foolishly I went on to tax with Gates, which was too earnest and dull. I should have asked him how on earth he'd become so rich! I should also have asked him what it was like to invent a game-changer like Microsoft from his garage – the kind of questions that viewers want to hear. The interview was in no way a disaster, but in retrospect I could have done a much better job on it. I kept my current affairs hat on for it and asked him, 'Why give all this money to charity when you could just pay tax? Why are you playing God?' Now, Bill Gates has done great work, on malaria in particular, but if I had opened the interview out, it would have been much better.

Needless to say, I learned a lot on *Morning Edition* – it was so different from what I'd been doing before – but I'd always liked live TV. The trouble was, the audiences for the programme remained low and it was an expensive show to put on, in spite of our tight budget. So almost two years later, the programme ended. I've never felt any bitterness when things like this happen. In TV, you've got to try a lot of things; it's a creative business, and some things will work and others won't. Putting on a dedicated news magazine programme in a small country was probably always going to be risky, but we gave it our best shot. By the end of our run, Anthony was completely wiped out: he'd put so much into the programme. I thought I was tired, but he was utterly exhausted. Now Anthony is Programme Editor of TV News and it has been fantastic to be working with him again as well as forming a new team with Caitríona Perry.

❧

Uncertainty is very much part of the game in broadcasting. You can be the hot new thing one week and yesterday's news the next. I'm well aware of that and I'm also well aware that I've had such a long and happy career at RTÉ. I consider it family, and so many of my colleagues have become good and trusted friends. RTÉ has been my rock during all my treatment and I know that, while my family comes first, it's 'home' to me now. It was hard to leave it, but it's going to be harder still to leave Conor on his own with Ben and Lucy. I'm a planner, but no amount of advance warning can prepare them for me not being there, that I know.

When my cancer returned in 2016, it was the beginning of a new period of uncertainty to which I'd have to adjust. We all had to. We were living in a rented house, having had to flee our dream home in Dún Laoghaire once the autumn winds started whipping in through the rickety windows and the holes in the roof. Our builders wouldn't be able to start working on it for another couple of months. Half our stuff was in storage and the other half was piled up in one of the rooms, gathering dust and occasional pigeon droppings from the birds that often found their way in, driving Dougal mad – and Conor too, as it was his job to shoo them out.

The rented house was cold, too, and I have to admit it was a pretty miserable time. Ben and Lucy were older, seven and ten respectively, and there was no hiding things from them then. Because my cancer was at stage 4, I could be fairly certain that I would live for another two years. Incredibly, my family at RTÉ took a chance on me and offered me the job of newsreader on the *Six One News*. That felt like such a huge vote of confidence in me, in spite of my illness. *Six One* was immense fun and another learning curve: it felt like such a boost to be learning new skills at this stage in my career, such as how to handle a five-minute interview, how to get the really important questions in and when, and how to respond to a moving news situation. I learned a lot from watching pros like Bryan Dobson and the late Marian Finucane. They just have 'it', that natural broadcaster's talent. The rest of us – well, we try!

Caitríona and I immediately hit it off. We were both learning on the job, for a start. Caitríona had come from being RTÉ's Washington Correspondent, which involves a different set of skills to news presenting, and I had been used to a different pace on *Morning Edition*, where I had more space to tell stories. There was a bond between us because neither of us had actually chased this fabulous job that we found ourselves doing. Also, we'd both started the job while undergoing big life changes. We both wanted to make this job our own and bring something new to it. And we were making history – the first two women to do the job as a team – which meant a lot to me. As a journalist, I've never felt the need to bang a drum, but seeing more women in positions of responsibility in media is fantastic – we are role models for the next generation, too, the

Lucys of the world, who will hopefully see us and be inspired.

We would take it in turns to do the big interview every night at 6.20, and being very collegiate, we'd always help each other out. If I had a hospital appointment, Caitríona would do the background to the interview so I could just glide in and go on air. Sometimes, after treatment, I'd be happily coasting along thanks to the steroids and Caitríona would ask me if I was feeling all right – I'd be feeling great! That's the only benefit of these drugs – they give you a temporary bump. But her kindness and instinctive desire to help was so brilliant.

In terms of the programme, our partnership worked seamlessly. From our daily trips to the make-up department at lunchtime for the application of the first layer of three, to the fun we had in wardrobe, we just got along. So much so that if one of us was seen without the other, it would be noted! After make-up and the first of the day's news conference meetings at 2.30 to discuss the stories of the day, we'd repair to the coffee dock or out to the sunshine if the weather was good and toss around a few ideas for that night's programme. We were working, I hasten to add, even if we had great fun doing it. Then it was back inside to begin the hard work of getting the interviews together, making calls and pinning sources down.

Our interview prep would continue right up until the minute we went live with it. Because it's basically such a short timeframe for an interview – a mere five minutes – time is a real issue. The biggest challenge is structuring it in such a way that you can get straight to the meat of it. No faffing and no filling airtime with information we already know. For example, if I ask the Minister for Transport, 'Why did the railway bridge not get built?', the answer will be something along the lines of, 'Oh, budget overruns, staffing problems and so on ...' People will already know this, so instead I'd open with, 'Now, Minister, earlier today you said that the bridge hadn't been built because of budget overruns and staffing problems ...' So I'd take the preamble away and say, 'The key question is this ...' When you give an open question first, the answer can eat up two minutes of the time. When I started on the *Six*, I had to really concentrate on the structure because it would be the opposite of that in documentary interviews:

they're open-ended; you keep going until you get what you want. However, in no way are we trying to get at anyone or attack them – we simply want the information that the viewer will want to know. And besides, nobody is interested in what I think of a certain politician – my opinions are not needed on the news. People are just interested in getting answers to pressing questions.

Another aspect of news reading is authority. In broadcasting, you either have authority in the studio or you don't. You can be an absolute terror outside the studio, but if you have authority on air, that's all that's required. I can still remember a time when it was thought that only men had this natural authority. I wonder if they'd ever seen Olivia O'Leary in action. She has tremendous authority. I don't think there's ever been anyone as good as her, and she came from an era when there were no women in news – she was just phenomenal. However, I seem to recall that even she noted that a certain forcefulness was a necessary tactic in interviews and I think that's one thing that has changed in broadcasting. It's less gladiatorial these days and this may have to do with the increased representation of women, but it's probably also down to changing styles. The default used to be that politicians were on no account to be trusted and the interviewer had to take them down, but now the focus is much more on getting answers. And the softly, softly approach works just as well, often better.

I was always struck by the calm that would descend in the studio just before we went to air. After the previous hour's frantic last-minute checks, the donning of the gúnas, the fitting of mics and earpieces, the pinning down of the running order, the rehearsal of timings with graphics, we'd stand in our opening camera positions, all the while exchanging snippets of gossip. As we chatted, Make-up would be checking us for shiny faces or loose threads. The editor would say 'Stop talking' and we'd obey as the opening credits rolled. The gallery – where the studio director and producer sit – would be keeping the show running and helping us, a wall of chatter and mild chaos while we presented a calm face to the nation. It helps to have had some experience of live TV, I've found. It means that no matter what's going on in the background, I can remain calm – or at least give the impression of remaining calm. Chaos could be breaking out in the background, but we had to say 'Good evening' and reassure the nation, no matter what was happening.

I can clearly remember the CervicalCheck controversy because the story would change even as we were on air, with new pieces of information emerging by the minute. Caitríona or I might be about to interview the Taoiseach or the Minister for Health, and suddenly a new piece of information would emerge that would change everything. We'd have to change the whole structure of our story and start again during the programme. The science of it was fascinating, even while the human story of the women involved and their families was so tragic. Because I understood the science, I felt that I could ask more pertinent questions about lab testing and the more technical aspects of the story. It gave me no pleasure to put pressure on ministers, but I knew it had to be done because the public needed to know.

The other story that affected me hugely was the Eighth Amendment. Regardless of my opinions on the subject – and they have nothing to do with my professional life – the debate was so polarising. I found that I had to really think hard before every single interview, because nobody would be fully happy with it. I had to steer a careful course between all sides of the debate and listen to terribly sad and difficult stories. Reporting from Donegal Town on the last day of media coverage before the referendum, I was doing the last two main interviews on each side, the pro-life and the pro-choice. I wanted those interviews to be clear – to take the heat and the emotion out of the debate and to answer straight-forwardly the toughest moral questions. To be fair to both Peter Boylan and Niamh Mhic Mhathúna, both tried to provide full answers to the public to enable them to decide.

I was so moved by the courage of all those who shared their experiences with the nation and I also felt that it was so interesting to look at Ireland at a time of huge change. Way back in my early years, when I was reviewing films and talking about pop culture, Ireland was such a different place. Many might bemoan the loss of certain values, but whatever your opinion, it was riveting to see how much our nation has changed in the last thirty years. What journalist wouldn't want to have a ringside seat during this time? It also struck me that a lot of the discourse on the issue was quite civil – not all of it, now – but maybe it was a sign of our coming of age that we were able to debate the issues in a more grown-up way, apart from a few ugly exceptions.

But Caitríona and I also had fun, it has to be said! During the ad breaks, when we had an interview guest in studio and they were getting their microphone on, we'd engage in a bit of small talk to relax them. One day, weatherman Gerry Murphy had come in to talk about one of the recent storms that had hit the country. Gerry was all business, suggesting questions and technical points. I listened intently to him talking about high-pressure patterns and isobars, then asked him the question that had been on my mind all along. 'Gerry, what I really want to know is – would you go on next year's *Dancing with the Stars*?'

Gerry, in all seriousness, thought about it before replying, 'Oh, I don't know, I'd have to be asked.'

'You'd be great on it,' I insisted. 'Why don't you think about it?' Caitríona burst out laughing as the music played us out of the ad break. Then it was 'five seconds to air', so the serious faces descended again and it was on with the show and our interview about the storm.

I can also remember the two of us sneaking into the sound check for the *Late Late Show* one Friday evening when they were rehearsing a tribute to country singer Big Tom. We stood up in the lighting gantry above the studio and sang along with all the country classics, 'Country Road', 'Rhinestone Cowboy' and so on. We could hear the producer in our earpieces saying, 'Where are Caitríona and Keelin? We need to rehearse the headlines.' We scooted off and ran into studio, fibbing about having left something up in wardrobe, whereupon the whole gallery erupted in laughter. We'd left our mics on and our entire sing-along had been heard by everyone.

And after the show? We'd do it all over again, but not before I received my nightly text messages from Dad and Ben. Dad would always text me to tell me that I'd done a great interview and Ben would set me straight on something I'd forgotten – or tell me that my dress was lovely! Caitríona's first question after the show would be, 'Well, what did your dad say?' He was our bellwether. I loved getting those texts, that reassurance that I was doing a good job, from the people who mattered most – my family.

CHAPTER 9

ALL IS LOST
END NOVEMBER 2019

Until June of 2019, I felt fine. I could feel queasy after chemo, but I had my supply of anti-nausea tablets, even if I did get sick sometimes after being on air. I can still remember telling Janice about it and she said she could run up the road to the studio and give me an injection to stop it. I can just see her, in her gorgeous dresses and shoes, trotting up Nutley Lane, a syringe in her hand! But then, suddenly, it was all over. Suddenly, I wasn't dashing in to work any more. I had joined the land of the unwell. And suddenly, Conor was looking after me full time and that took some getting used to. I had to develop a more-than-usual amount of elasticity to adapt to my new life and to do so without making everyone else's life a misery.

I'm proud of what I achieved in my working life. It's so tempting to shrug our shoulders at the problems of the world, which can seem over-whelming, but I feel lucky that I was able to do even something small to address them. Even though I loved the fun and excitement of *Six One*, my heart was always in documentaries. Often I'd think of all the ordinary people I'd met, trying to deal with the stuff of life in incredibly difficult circumstances. I was lucky enough to meet people whose interior lives were as rich and varied as my own, but whose life choices were restricted by poverty. I often think about that early programme on St Teresa's Gardens. It's always stayed in my mind because of the extraordinary people I met. A mind-boggling 87 per cent of the residents were on social welfare and problems like drug addiction, mental health issues and domestic violence were endemic. I remember one young man, who'd been in and out of jail for years, telling me that he thought he'd be in again before too long because it was 'a bit of a break'. Then there was Donna, a mum of five, who was on methadone dispensed by a local clinic. She had €70 a week to spend after paying her utility bills – to cover groceries, clothes and shoes for five children. She was surviving on visits from the local St Vincent de Paul and vouchers to buy the kids clothes. She hadn't been out for a night in eight years because she had no money for a social life, and when I asked her what she imagined her future being, she replied that she didn't see one.

Wendy was another resident, a young woman with a toddler, who had successfully battled heroin addiction and who was now 'only' on antidepressants. The story she told us, of the frustration and boredom of her life, stayed with me and I was terribly sad to hear that she died just two weeks after we'd filmed her. Her baby was found with her body and it was thought he'd been there for two days.

The St Teresa's Gardens complex has now been demolished and the site cleared to build new social housing. I sometimes wonder what happened to the rest of the people I met when we filmed there. Where did they end up and what kind of lives are they living?

Of course, there were also comical moments working on the documentaries and reports I did. Ceddy – Cedric Culleton – and I made a documentary on the Chamber Street flats in the Liberties as part of a series on social inequality in Ireland, and we ended up visiting a woman in her sixties, who I'll call Nora, who used to hold karaoke sessions in her flat with her friends every day. For about a week, we lived in a parallel universe where we'd call into her in the morning and then her two friends would arrive. They were younger guys, I'd say in their thirties, and they'd come off heroin and were now on methadone and alcohol, which is a common replacement. They'd sit there all day with the curtains closed, singing away. Every now and then they'd say, 'All right, I'm going on a run.' A 'run' was taking Nora's tartan shopping trolley to the off-licence to fill it up with cans of Dutch Gold. When they returned, they'd all start drinking. And then, they'd begin to sing. One of the lads would get up and do an AC/DC number, but Nora preferred old folk songs, like 'Down by the Salley Gardens'. It was bizarre, perhaps, but understandable, as they considered it to be too dangerous to leave the flat much, apart from their 'runs'. Conor and I called up to them on Christmas Day with a voucher for Dunnes Stores to find the flat just as it was every other day of the year: curtains drawn, no tree, no decorations. There was no Christmas because, in a sense, every day was Christmas Day. There was no structure in their lives: no job, no education, no nothing. Just the drink, the music and each other. It was tragic and comic at the same time. The real pity was that we couldn't find a spot for it in the documentary, but I'll never forget it.

I'm not sure if I understand just why I'm thinking about those people right now – maybe because I've been thinking about resilience and wondering whether it's possible to 'bounce back' from deprivation. It's not a simple question of overcoming life's hurdles – what if they are just too big or require too much effort? What if the playing field isn't level? Thinking about this makes me put my own struggles in perspective, even though, to me, they feel so real. I'm not the only person to have faced them and I won't be the last. I'm not special in that sense, but that doesn't stop me hoping that I'll be the one to buck the trend, to overcome my cancer and to just keep on going.

The news comes from the US via email in the end. I couldn't believe they didn't call me, but Janice says she knows why: they need to spell it out so that I understand – so that there can be no ambiguity. I am no longer a candidate for the treatment. There it is, plain and simple.

∂෴෴

Conor once told me about the 'all-is-lost' moment in filmmaking. It was during our last 'proper' summer holiday, in 2018. We took the ferry to France and drove to a tiny village near Le Mans in northern France, famous for its 24-hour race, and such a pretty place. We'd booked an Airbnb for a week before taking an extended route back, spending a few days in Roscoff, then taking a ferry to Plymouth and on to Wales. Finally, we'd head home on the ferry from Holyhead. I think Conor wanted us to share as many family moments as possible, but by the time we got to Plymouth none of us were talking. The weather was bad, everyone was hungry and grumpy and Lucy had a headache. We went on a big trek to find a restaurant but it was late and everywhere was closing. We marched back to the hotel and ate in the bar there, still glum.

Then Conor said, 'It's okay, we're just having our "all-is-lost" moment. In just about every good film, the hero experiences a point when things have just got worse and worse and suddenly it looks like all is lost – no way are they going to get out of this one… But then something happens to turn things around and the goodies prevail. We're having our all-is-lost moment now.' He was right. The next day came and the skies were blue and we drove through the glorious countryside to a converted barn on a little farm in Llyswen, just over the Welsh border. I can still remember standing in the evening light. Ben was lying in a hammock, reading, Conor was putting more wood on the firepit and Lucy was feeding the goat that lived in the next field. All was not lost.

❧

But now I'm in with Janice and the palliative care doctor, Brendan, and we look blankly at the email from NIH in the US. 'Hi Keelin, we're really sorry, we're not going to be able to continue any treatment, because it's no longer safe with the presence of cancer in your spinal fluid.'

That was it. No pep talk, no 'nice to have met you', no recognition of just what this email was going to do to me and my family.

'What's going on?' I asked Brendan and Janice. 'What does it mean, they can't continue any treatment? I don't understand.'

Janice said, 'I totally understand it,' and she tried to explain to me exactly what having cancer in my spinal fluid meant. 'It's just too dangerous.'

I had always thought 'the end of the line' would be more dramatic somehow than sitting in a room in St Vincent's Hospital. For so many months, I had hung on to this shard of hope. I thought of the American woman whose cancer had been reversed and who was now happily kayaking and hiking around the place. I wanted to be that woman, to be able to start my life again, to swim in the Forty Foot, to do ordinary things like go to IKEA to buy shelves for my utility room, or take Dougal for a walk down the pier, or have a chat with the kids without them having to call up to my room and lie on the bed beside me to tell me about their day. I don't want much, I really don't. But this email has given me another version of my life: one where I will slide downhill, either quickly or slowly, until I fade away, disappear.

Later that day, my sister Niamh comes to visit me. She's a nurse, so she's familiar with the lingo, and as she helps me to adjust my pillows, I blurt, 'What's going to happen, Niamh?'

She continues fluffing up the pillows, tears in her eyes that she doesn't want me to see. Finally, she says, 'Keelin, you're going to get better than you are today. You're not going to be like this all of the time, but you are getting weaker now and you will continue to get weaker and we're going to have to find a way through it. We'll find a way to cope.'

I cling to her certainty for the rest of the afternoon, that somehow I'll find a way to cope with this news. That we'll find a way, Conor and myself. But first, we have to tell the kids. How do you tell your children that you're going to die? It's a question few of us will have to answer. I will have to tell them, but first, I need to come to terms with it myself. It's a funny thing, to suggest that you can somehow get used to the idea of dying, but you can. You'd be surprised.

I can still remember the overwhelming feeling of shock when I was first diagnosed with cancer in

2011. I walked around in a daze for days, trying to comprehend what I'd been told. It wasn't just the physical side of things, although that was certainly a consideration; it was the understanding that life was going to change. I'd always had a clear picture of what the future might look like. But after my diagnosis, I found that this picture needed to change. I had assumed that I would see the children grow up; that I'd grow old with Conor; that I would become a granny; that there would be plenty of holidays with my sister Emma and her children; plenty of time to read the news and to laugh with my colleagues at work, as well as to grill politicians or interview well-known people; cook all those recipes I'd earmarked in the *Feast* supplement that comes with *The Guardian* every weekend. Suddenly, I wasn't sure of my future any more. When I recovered, the following year, the picture began to come into focus again: I was back at work, my hair was mine again (although it had grown back curly and for a while I was going around like Rizzo, the tough-talking, pregnant one in *Grease*). Aged just four and two, the children were unaware of the true implications of cancer: their little lives would continue unchanged.

I can still remember lying on the trampoline with them one sunny summer day during my first cancer treatment; as they bounced up and down, I lay there watching the clouds, soaking up the sun. It was utterly blissful, largely because I knew that no matter what was going on for me, life was as happy for them as it always had been.

Experts tell you that coming to terms with cancer involves 'tolerating uncertainty' and I suppose they're right. In the time between my first diagnosis and my second, five years, I learned to live with the shadow of it, telling myself that the odds were good, the statistics were on my side and the rest I'd leave in the lap of the gods. I put all thoughts of cancer out of my mind. I didn't fully close the door on it, but I did move on from it and back into life again.

But after going to America, it was a slow descent, even with the promise of the new trial. Now, I have to prepare my children for the worst, to give them the time to take the enormity of it on board. I urgently need to be honest with them so that they can begin the process of grieving. It's tempting to fantasise that they'll somehow be happier not knowing, but I know that's not true. A friend of mine once told me that when her mother died unexpectedly when my friend was a child, she thought that she had done something to make it happen. She had spent the rest of her life blaming herself. I don't want that for Ben and Lucy.

We decide to tell them in the hospital because I don't want to pollute the house with the news. 'Pollute' might be a strong word, but I know that if I tell them at home, every time they sit on the couch in the living room, they'll remember.

We bring them in to my room on Cedar Ward and I say, 'I'm going to have to tell you something – the American trial has been cancelled.'

Lucy understands it immediately. 'Is that it? So, when are you doing to die?'

I say, 'Look, Lucy, nobody knows; it will be sooner rather than later, it might be Christmas, who knows? We might even get to next summer.' I know that that probably isn't realistic, because Janice has told me as much, but it just gives her space to process it. Poor Ben, he just bursts into tears and says, 'I don't want to talk about this.' Of course he doesn't, and I don't push him. I know that it has been terrible enough for one day, and that I can follow up by introducing the idea gently to them over the next days and weeks. I also know that no matter how hard it is, I have to keep telling them the truth. If I don't, their trust in me and Conor will be broken.

I need to somehow make this process 'normal' for them, whatever that really means. It breaks my heart, though, that these two wonderful children are not going to have their mother. It's not about me – every child needs their mother – but I also know that I have no choice in the matter. None of us has. Conor is an amazing father and husband, but I often wonder what life will be like for them in the house without me. Sometimes I imagine that it'll be kind of like *The Young Ones*. It'll be a household of equals, even Dougal the dog. The dynamic will change, I know. Now, maybe more than ever, we parents are a unit in the face of the kids, but when I die, the situation will reverse. Conor and Ben can bicker, but without me, they'll have to sort things out themselves – and I worry how that will resolve itself. And Lucy, who has only just begun secondary school, will have to do all her exams, her growing up, without me by her side. Now they are on a journey, to process grief. They're not talking to us about it, but that doesn't mean that they are not feeling it and trying to work out what it all means. Sometimes it just seems too big to contemplate, but at other times, I know that making it manageable, sharing each step of the way with them, is the right thing to do.

CHAPTER 10

SWINGS AND ROUNDABOUTS
CHRISTMAS AND NEW YEAR 2019–20

It's the darkest time of the year and a gloom settles on the little park across the road. It's more or less deserted now apart from the odd dog walker, standing on the damp grass, watching a dog pace around. My tree is bare, the branches dark against the leaden sky. It's all a bit depressing and the murky weather matches my mood. It's not like me. Christmas is coming and I've always been in love with the festive season. However, I'm distracted by pain due to the PICC line they put in me last week. PICC is short for 'peripherally inserted central catheter', which is a bit of a mouthful. Even though I've resisted it until now, my veins have proved to be my weak spot and the nurses are finding it harder and harder to get a line in, so I've had to give in. The PICC is basically a long, thin tube that has been inserted in my arm and that winds its way to my heart so that they can draw blood and administer meds without having to dig around in my arm. It's excruciatingly painful right now. The site in my upper arm is throbbing in spite of the padding around the catheter. I vow to give it a week and see if it settles. But it leaves me grizzly and irritable.

My oldest friend, journalist Nicola Byrne, has agreed to help me make notes on my life for my book because I can't write for long, and she comes in this morning, looking glamorous in a furry jacket, wide-legged trousers and trainers, her hair freshly blow-dried. She looks lovely, full of life, and even though I'm wearing my beloved stripy top and a comfy pair of trousers, I know that I can't indulge myself in fashion any more. I have a double wardrobe full of cool skirts, colourful tops and some gorgeous dresses that I have accumulated over the years and I feel a bit wistful about not being able to wear any of it. I need loose clothing and layers to stay warm, so it's all practical. Still, I can admire her and we share a laugh as we settle down to chat.

We're in the sitting room in front of a roaring log burner, and we giggle away as we recount our utter boldness as teenagers. We were always getting into scrapes and our 'trip to Knock' has become family legend. Mum and Dad were going away for the weekend and Nicola and I were to join a school trip to Knock. However, we had other ideas – there must have been a party planned – and we arranged to meet up once the coast was clear. Nicola's parents smelled a rat when they saw her best party outfit hidden in her overnight bag, so she rushed up to the phone box in Howth, where she lived, to warn me that her mum was going to call mine, and would discover that neither of my parents was at home. Conor and his friend Conor O'Brien were there at the time and I said, 'One of you will have to pretend to be my dad on the phone.' Conor O'Brien, who had recently played Fagin in a school production of *Oliver Twist*, was happy to oblige, even though he sounded nothing like Derry. 'It's a very bad line,

Tina. But I can assure you there will be harsh words. Good luck, now!' Somehow we got away with it!

Nicola and I had met on our first day of secondary school, in Loreto on the Green, and we were instantly friends. I think we're kindred spirits: we share the same sense of humour, and we are both gentle boundary-pushers. We made our first steps into the working world together and we're both journalists. While I went into the world of broadcasting, Nicola carved out a very successful career, starting on Vincent Browne's *Dublin Tribune*, then moving to South Africa and reporting from there. Indeed, she made the news herself in 1996 when Mary Robinson made a state visit to meet Nelson Mandela. Nicola was among the assembled press and Mandela went to greet them. As he shook Nicola's hand, he asked her if she was married, adding that if he wasn't married himself he might be tempted to propose to her. Anyway, she has always been my closest friend and she will look out for Conor. She will get him out of himself. I have great faith in her.

I'm expecting more comfy chat about what my children call 'the olden days', but the tone shifts as

Nicola puts her sharp, probing journalist's hat on, asking me questions about how I feel about my life, my cancer. I'm finding it tough going. I was never one for navel gazing or sitting at a rainy window pondering the meaning of life. So pouring my heart and soul out doesn't come naturally to me. But I've been spending rather a lot of time recently doing both! When you're dying, as I am, you think a lot about the process, practically and spiritually. You think about the life you've had, and about leaving it all behind. You think about your children.

I'm a practical woman, so I've also been giving a lot of thought to my funeral. I have the undertaker booked, the same one who looked after Mum, and I know that my funeral will take place in St Paul's Church in Glenageary. I have also bought matching urns for my ashes. I know that this might seem morbid, but I want to make everything normal for Conor and the children. I don't want death to be a huge drama for them all, full of pain. I want it to be as natural as possible, in spite of everything. The urns come from an auction house. I only need one, but they have arrived in a lot with two Aynsley lamps that I've passed on to a friend's mother, and now they sit downstairs, either side of the fireplace, ready for use.

Purchasing the urns came with its own dark comedy. Conor and I had both set up accounts to bid online and at one point I think we may have put in a bid against each other. We went and collected them from the auction house, which might seem odd given my infirmity, but setting about practical tasks is a great help at times like this. About a week later, Conor got a call from the same auction house asking when he might pick up the table. He wondered if I had bought it as a surprise Christmas present, but it turned out he had accidentally bid for it with the slip of a finger. When Conor explained his mistake, the auctioneer was quite incredulous. When the man revealed that the price tag was €1,200, poor Conor had to 'bring out the big guns', as he put it, and explain that his wife had stage 4 cancer and that he had enough to worry about without spending such a sum on a table he had nowhere to put anyway. 'Then there's no point continuing this discussion,' said the auctioneer, and he hung up.

'You're a hero,' I told my husband, taking his hand.

'Perhaps. But also an idiot,' he replied.

I like the idea of my ashes being next to the fire, nice and warm, close to my family. I don't want to be put somewhere freezing, far away from home. I want to feel that I'm still close to the people I love the most. I've managed to write down some pages to Lucy and Ben in two little notebooks I bought for the purpose. I scratch my head as I try to think of the right words to tell them how much I love them. I feel the responsibility of saying just the right thing to them, knowing that they'll open these notebooks from time to time and hoping that when they do, they'll remember me and be consoled by my words. I want to tell them that even though I'm gone, I'll always be there for them. All they have to do is to think of me. I also find myself reminding them to do their homework, stop bickering and brush their teeth twice a day. Being a mum means looking after the practicals too. Luckily, Conor took photos *everywhere* we went, so I think they have a good archive of memories to draw from.

It turns out that dying also involves a lot of admin. If I died and left a bank account in my name only, it would be frozen until probate went through and my pension would be paying into a frozen account. So Conor and I went to the bank in Dún Laoghaire and asked them to close some existing accounts and open new joint ones. It was a strange meeting, not least for the poor young manager sitting behind her desk, all perfect hair and make-up. She helped us sort it all out but we both felt suddenly very, very old. I also have money tucked away in the post office – and I had to sort it out, because I'd lost the book and I wanted to withdraw the cash. I had to do a will, too. I hate admin, as, I'm sure, does everyone else, but I know it's essential: my dying is bad enough without leaving Conor with a tangle of legal stuff to sort out.

The preparations have also provided us with un-intended amusement. One day, we were all sitting in the car when Lucy piped up, 'Hey, Mum, are you going to leave us any money?' There's honesty for you. I said, 'I suppose I will, if you want me to.' I think that as much as she might have liked a bit of cash – what teenager doesn't? – she was also trying to understand just what my death might mean for her and for Ben and Conor. I'm not sure if she realises the permanence of it, that I'll be going and never coming back. I most certainly do, and when I allow myself to think about it, a wave of fear and sadness washes over me. So the practical things help me to keep focused and not let my emotions get the better of me. Of course I'm scared, but if the kids see that, they'll be scared too.

I don't have a particular religious faith, so my funeral will be a secular one, but I do believe that we live on in how we've been in life, in people's memories of us, and also in those who come after us. I know that because I can hear my mother in me all the time, and I see her in Lucy. I also have so many memories of her. She was never happier than when she had the whole family round for Sunday lunch. She'd manage to find a gap among all the voices talking across each other and say, 'Isn't this just lovely!' She really knew how to enjoy the moment – and she loved a good laugh! She gave birth to me in Indianapolis in 1968, not too long after Dad had got a job there. It was a great time to be in America and she loved being there. I think it had a big influence on her – all that can-do positivity. She believed in her children and didn't try to push us one way or another – although I sometimes think we could have done with a bit more nudging. Dad was always very busy at work, and there was a lot of hosting dinners for visiting academics to be done. She wasn't a big fan of fancy cooking but she would just get the big cookbook out, get everyone well fed and she'd join in the chat. When I look at my siblings, I can see her in all of them. And I remember, the first Christmas after she died, when Lucy was just a few months old, Conor said how much of her he saw in me. Most young women, I know, would reject the idea of being like their mothers. But I think all of us are happy to embrace it in the end, as I was.

Looking back, I feel that I'm terribly lucky to have had an entirely 'normal' adolescence and I'm conscious of the south County Dublin bubble in which I was brought up. My best friends are those I made in school and if it weren't for *Prime Time*, I suspect I would have remained a Southside girl, in spite of all the years we lived in the city, first in that lovely apartment on Pembroke Street, followed by an awful, dingy place off Synge Street, a house near the Royal Canal Basin, an apartment in the charming Mespil Buildings off Leeson Street, then our first little house in Rialto, followed by the Victorian doer-upper on the South Circular Road ...

I remember going to meet the girls from school –
Nicola, Fiona, Kyla, Debbie and Taffina – for drinks
at the Clarence Hotel one night. I was walking down
the Quays towards the entrance, when I bumped into
a young man, 'Karl', whom I'd met a couple of years
before. We'd been making a programme on teenage
prostitution and he was one of our subjects, a rent
boy who, when he became too old for his punters, at
around sixteen, was tasked with spotting vulnerable
youngsters in games arcades and luring them into
the business. His story was desperately sad: one of
three boys, he didn't share the same father and was
an outcast in the family and ended up prostituting
himself for money. I can still remember him coming
out to the studio to be interviewed. We were going
to dress him differently so he wouldn't be recognised
on camera, and in the dressing room, he spotted that
there was a bathroom. 'Can I have a shower?' he said
in a small voice.

Now he appeared before me, waving hello. We
stood there chatting for a few minutes as the wind
whipped down the river, the kind of small talk you
make with an acquaintance when you bump into
them. Then we parted, me in my glossy work gear

to the Clarence, him to God knows what. I have no idea what became of him, but it struck me that there is such a fine line dividing us, such a narrow gap between a happy life full of possibilities and a tragic one of shame and rejection. It wasn't fair. It isn't fair. And I'm well aware of that, and of the fact that none of us really does much about it.

I suppose I've been giving that a lot of thought while I go over my life in my head and with Nicola, discussing what's important and what I'll leave out: the stories and the experiences that have shaped me. I've been thinking about why the cards are dealt in a certain way and what we make of them, or whether our circumstances permit us to do so. I have met any number of people who I know would have gone on to do all kinds of interesting things, were it not for the toughness of their early lives. I became who I was largely because of my golden childhood and education, even if, at times, I didn't make the most of it, but I always had the choice. It was a given that I'd go to university and even though I graduated with a measly 2.2, due to a distinct lack of hard work, it was enough to give me the tools I needed in life.

Now, I wonder about Lucy and Ben. Conor and I were lucky enough to be able to give them the privileges that we'd had, and I feel cheated, quite honestly, out of seeing where they go in life. I wonder how they'll be when they grow older, if Lucy will lose that dreamy, sunny creativity, or Ben become less of a bundle of energy and ideas, and I wish that I could be there to see it because I think they will both make their mark, but I have to accept that I can't. I don't want to go to my resting place feeling angry and bitter and leaving my family with unhappy memories. I want to go smiling and hopefully joking, chatting away, the way I always have been.

I'm not dying yet, though, I know that. I haven't yet taken to the bed, not fully at least, and I can still shuffle around with my walking stick, even though my rattly chest is beginning to annoy me. Janice has been very straight with me. After the US trial failed, I said to her, 'Do you think I'll make Christmas?' She just replied, 'I'd be worried about you, Keelin.' I really admired her for that. You can't go around giving false hope – it's not fair. But the prospect of not being there for Christmas is hard. Will it mean the magic is ruined for the kids for ever?

Funnily enough, though, PICC line notwith-
standing, physically I'm on a little plateau at the
moment. I'm not declining further, thanks to the new
regime of Taxol chemotherapy. I don't think Janice
had high expectations for it, but recent blood tests
showed that my cancer markers have stabilised, so,
miracle of miracles, I've bought some time. I actually
don't feel too bad. Gradually, I'm feeling confident
that I will see one last Christmas after all. Nicola
has kindly brought home a lovely golden piglet
that I asked her to pick up when she was in Paris
for Conor's Christmas present. It will go with the
golden rabbit Conor got me when we were in Paris
for our friend Greg's wedding. I put it with the kids'
presents, which have been hidden away at the back
of my wardrobe.

I'm quite enjoying the view from my plateau.
I'm aware of the fact that the house is slightly in
limbo, waiting to see what will happen to me and
when. Life has been abnormal for six months now
and part of me would love to see my family return
to their lives once more. Everyone's on hold until I
die – especially Conor, who is looking after me full
time at the moment. He hasn't been out much in

months, apart from his driving lessons, but he just keeps on going and he never makes me feel guilty. I think many people with cancer feel that they are being a burden to their families – I know I do – with the constant flow of needs: more water (with more ice in it this time), another can of Diet Coke, almost daily trips to the pharmacy for one thing or another. It must be tiring. But when I've said it to him, he says, 'Oh God, how can you even think that way? I want you to be happy and enjoy being looked after. You've earned it.' He even got me a big TV for our bedroom instead of using my rubbish laptop. I've been able to get to the end of a French TV show on Netflix called *Call My Agent*, which I really enjoyed. It's funny and very French. I'm also really enjoying *Veep*, *Grace and Frankie* and *Better Call Saul*. *The Crown* is brilliant and I hope I get to the end of it before I go. Conor says I need to hang on for at least a couple of months to get through all the 'brilliant' (i.e. challenging!) stuff that he's recorded on the Sky box. We'll see.

I wonder if one day I'll think, Okay, I'm dying now – or if I'll even be aware of it. I don't know if I'll experience the moment of death, because most people I've seen at the moment of death are deeply comatose. But as I go into that coma, I wonder if I'll know that I'm turning that corner that I'm not coming back from. I've had a lot of ups and downs and so far, I've come back from all of them. When I came back from America in June, I had lost a huge amount of weight and took to my bed for a few weeks, but I bounced back. In November, I was very sick again, around the time that I heard about the US trial. I really thought that it was over for me then. But each time, I've had a little boost in my health to keep me going. I know I'm probably running out of that now, with the amount of cancer I have. I'd like to get to the end of February, to the brighter days, the shift that can sometimes come in early spring – followed by a month of rain and maybe a bit of snow! I would love even just to see green buds appear on my tree and have a sense of new life beginning. You never know. But the other day I had a visit from Laura, the lovely nurse from Our Lady's Hospice in Blackrock, to talk about the final few weeks and days, and I said, brightly, that I might get to the end of February. Laura gave me a doubtful look. I suppose she's seen a lot of this, but I choose to keep on hoping, because I'd love just a bit of warm light. Sometimes I feel like my tree, leaning towards the sunlight, soaking up every ray.

I don't feel fear about death. Maybe I will when I'm right up against it, I don't know, but I don't think so. I'm dying of cancer, I'm not dying of thirst in a desert, or in a road traffic accident where I can see the blood draining out of me. I will be managed, I will be minded, I'll have pain relief. Nobody wants to die, but this way it won't be difficult. It won't leave my family in chaos – one moment you're there and the next you're gone. This way, I have time to come to terms with it, we all do.

In the meantime, it's almost Christmas and Lucy and Ben are rehearsing one of their plays that they regularly put on with their cousins. Lucy has adapted the script from the short film *Angela's Christmas* – which was based on a story that Frank McCourt's mother, Angela, used to tell him when he was a child. Angela kidnaps the baby Jesus from his cold crib in the church and brings him home to warm him up. Lucy is writing her own stage version and there are lots of fights about who gets what role, and as I sit on the sofa, I can hear the rehearsals going on upstairs. I'm so glad that they still want to do this kind of thing; that even though Lucy is thirteen and Ben eleven, they are still children, not quite ready to begin to grow up and reject their parents, or staying glued to their mobiles all day. If I don't get to see the performance itself, it doesn't matter – it's enough to hear their happy chatter and raucous laughter echoing through the house. It's life going on, just as it should be.

CHAPTER 11

INTO A NEW YEAR
MID-JANUARY 2020

At last, there's a little more brightness in the day. I can feel it as I turn my head to the sun. It's still weak, but it's most definitely a tiny bit warmer – and, as we'd joke as soon as it got to New Year's Day, 'there's a grand stretch in the evening'. The day *is* a little longer: the sun is setting half an hour later than it did in the gloom of midwinter. I know this because I am able to study the sunset from the window of my hospital room, where I've been spending more time recently as the illness progresses. Down below, in the garden of the nursing home next door, there's a squirrel scampering about, watched – at some distance – by a cat that's hunkered down in the grass. But the instincts of self-preservation are strong in the humble squirrel. Curious and hungry it may be, but it never wanders far from the safety of a tree.

You can get lost in these moments. Or maybe it's the effect of the painkillers, although they don't zonk me out like they did a few months back. It takes a while to establish exactly the best programme of drugs so that I'm not feeling much pain, but I'm still generally lucid. When I was ill after returning from America – back in July and August – I was on such a high dose of oxycodone that I was sleeping most of the day, and very groggy in between. All I could manage was episodes of *Call My Agent*, having to rewind constantly because I'd forgotten what was happening. I was very comfortable, I have to say, but I think the kids, and Conor, were starting to get a glimpse of what the future could be like: me being barely there, then being gone.

I have come back in to St Vincent's so that they can drain my lungs of the fluid that has been building up persistently inside them. What was a mild rattle has now become a full-blown wheeze and every time I inhale, I feel as if I'm drowning a little bit. It's not pleasant, so while I have the current batch drained, a procedure that results in a full two litres of fluid, Janice is looking into a more permanent solution. As far as I understand it, the fluid is in the sac that holds my lungs, the pleural lining, rather than in the lungs themselves, so the procedure involves collapsing the lungs and filling up the area with talc. Yes, talc. It's very absorbent, but it also helps to stick the lung to the pleural lining, so there's no space for fluid to accumulate. If the fluid can't go there, it'll be reabsorbed by the body. It sounds a bit medieval, but if it cures me of this awful sensation of not being able to draw a full breath, it'll be worth it. I think the operation takes about an hour, and if it works, I won't have to keep coming in to have my lungs drained.

I thought my terrible thirst would go away in here, but it hasn't. I feel as if I could drink a lakeful of water and I find myself asking the lovely staff for a refill of my jug every time they appear. I also find myself fixating on drinking Diet Coke or my lovely elderflower cordial, something sweet and refreshing. I don't know where the thirst comes from and Janice is a bit baffled, but it's driving me mad.

I've always been sanguine about the surgery I've had during both cancer experiences. The first time I needed a mastectomy, but if they'd told me I needed my left leg removed, I would have agreed to it. I opted to have a new breast made from my own tissue. While it was a longer ordeal than reconstruction with an implant – six weeks instead of two – it meant that I never had to undergo another procedure. In some women, the implant has to be replaced due to the build-up of scar tissue. I know that for many women, the loss of part of themselves is a big thing, but now, I can't help wondering if it made that much of a difference to me. I lived with a temporary prosthesis for a couple of years, which slipped into a pocket in a special bra, and that made me look fairly normal. Certainly, I didn't feel like an incomplete woman, and if I had my time again, I'm not sure I'd bother. I grew used to the new me and the scars that came with her. The interesting thing about that procedure is that it does produce a more natural breast, which curiously loses weight with the rest of me, which I find a bit odd. Still, it's just one of the many assaults on the body that cancer entails. I say this as an observation, not a moan!

As I look out of the window now, waiting to chat to one of the many doctors or nurses who appear by my bedside from time to time, a huddle of golfers ambles towards the green in the Elm Park golf course below. They are all brightly dressed in their *de rigueur* diamond-patterned jumpers and check trousers, like a flock of exotic birds. I like to watch them stride briskly across the grounds, all the while wondering to myself what it would be like to be able to be out and about like that in the waning evening sun, getting in one last hole before 'wine o'clock'. It's the thing I miss most about life: simple fresh air. I'm thinking about this as I drift off to sleep, propped up on my pillows.

The next day, I'm taken to the operating theatre for my procedure. I'm not really nervous about it because I've had surgery before, so I no longer worry about the unknown. I chat with the nurses to distract myself before being wheeled in to the operating theatre. I'm always amazed at how bright it is in there, with all the lights blasting, but there's also a spectacular view of the whole of Dublin Bay. The tide is out now and the muddy brown sand stretches for miles. Before we moved out to Dún Laoghaire we used to sometimes take Dougal there for a big run. He loves being by the sea almost as much as I do, and we had some lovely walks across the flats towards the red and white chimneys of Poolbeg. I drift off, thinking of wide open spaces and salty air.

❧

I wake up in the High Dependency Unit (HDU), with a drain fitted to draw off any post-op fluid and a terrible headache. The procedure has gone according to plan and I'm relieved to feel that I can breathe fully at last. But because I'm immuno-compromised, along with everything else, I have to stay in the HDU for three nights. It is impressive and the lovely nurses are brilliant, but it's so clinical compared to Cedar Ward, which has more or less become my home. I get quite frustrated with the slowness of it all, trying to distract myself with a bit of reading. But I find it hard to concentrate these days, so in the end I decide to bid on a dress ring on an auction website. It keeps me occupied! A neighbour of mine got a beautiful vintage ring from O'Reilly's on Francis Street a couple of months ago, so I've been keeping an eye out and spotted a lovely one. I call them and put down a bid of €200. The next day, like a child at Christmas, I call again and they tell me I've been successful – and for €160. Bargain! It's lovely: a big solid smoky topaz stone in a simple gold setting. As I say, big, but not too flashy. I was going to get them to post it to me here in the hospital, but Conor was in town recording a radio ad so he went and got it. A friend of mine says it might be 1960s, but I'm not that bothered about the age – it cheers me up every time I look at it. I hasten to add that I'm not on eBay every day of the week ordering things, I'm not a big shopper, but the distraction is very welcome.

I make it to the ward in the end, but my drain has started to produce a bit too much fluid and a crowd of doctors gathers to examine it and decide what to do about me. You have to be producing under 200ml a day to have a drain removed, and it was taking me a bit longer. Finally, two visions in blue scrubs walk through the door and say, 'It's coming out!' I have never been so excited as the consultant and the registrar fuss around me, getting ready to remove the drain. It feels like an alien coming out of me, a big, long snake of plastic tubing, but once it's gone, I feel better. Just the psychological boost of no longer having it there means so much to me. It feels as if I've overcome a big hurdle: a sign that I've come through it. Maybe, I think to myself, I can keep going for a little longer. But then I stop myself. Just live in the moment, Keelin. Live. In. The. Moment.

The other development in hospital is that I have my remaining hair shaved off. Grace, a friend of my sister Muireann, volunteered to come in and do it for me. She's a professional hairdresser, with the kindest manner, and that made it easier. But still, it's more traumatic than the first time because I know I'll never see my hair again. It needs to go for practical reasons – the stray hair has been finding its way all around the house – but when I'm handed a mirror to look at my newly bald head, I can't quite take it in. My eyes look huge under my bald scalp and the air around my ears feels cold. At least I still have my eyebrows and lashes. This must be how a baby feels, I think. Vulnerable, unable to fend for itself.

I have always sucked my thumb, while twiddling my hair, so I get her to make me a little pigtail for me to twiddle. I wonder, as I write, if this is too much information, but I find this habit so soothing: I go back to being a child again, sitting in front of the TV at home, my brother and sisters around me. Now all my sisters, and Lucy, are volunteering to donate hair. But because I'm newly bald in midwinter, I have gone online to order a couple of warm woolly caps. They're cashmere and, frankly, expensive, but I feel that I need the warmth and softness against my skin. I don't want anything prickly or itchy. I can remove them in hospital, where it's boiling, but also layer them when it's very cold.

∾౿∾

It's now a full two weeks after my operation and I've been home from hospital for a couple of days. No matter how many times I go in, I forget that getting out of hospital is always a bit of a production. It took me an entire day, with various visits from doctors, and my prescriptions. Part of me couldn't wait to get home, but another part of me knew that I'd miss it, in a way. In hospital, the only thing you have to think about is what to watch on telly, as you are minded by the nurses and food is produced every few hours, whether you need it or not. There are even two tea-and-biccy runs and with the lack of exercise, I've actually been putting on weight. I'm no longer worried about it because I've lost so much: my bones jut out and when I fall, which I do a bit these days, I really feel the lack of padding, so a little extra weight is a good thing. Mind you, I'd have loved to take a nurse home with me. As any long-term patient will tell you, returning home when you are sick isn't straightforward. You feel as if you're a burden to your family and you also feel vulnerable, having to look after yourself, worrying about every twinge. It's funny how quickly you become institutionalised.

This loss of independence doesn't sit well with me. Having grown up as the eldest of five, I suppose you get used to being top dog, in a way. I don't think I lorded over my siblings, but I'm sure I was a bossy big sister at times. I'm always being reminded of the night I kicked my sister Muireann out of the room we shared because she was coughing too much, but thankfully Muireann never held a grudge. She has been a regular visitor to my bedside, just checking in to see how I'm feeling. It's always great to see her. In fact, one of the blessings in all this is being reminded how amazing all my siblings are – Muireann, Eoin, Emma and Niamh. We've had plenty of time to go over the old memories. We always end up having a laugh, no matter how grim the circumstances. It was like this with Mum, and now here we all are again.

I was determined to get home, even though the simple act of packing my bag had slightly worn me out, because it was my twentieth wedding anniversary a couple of days later and Conor had booked a table in Michael's in Mount Merrion for lunch. I had been wanting to try it for ages, having heard great things about the place. There is no way I'm going to miss it, I thought as I climbed up the steps to the front door, home again. Twenty years is cause for celebration, particularly now.

Getting to the top of those steps was like getting to the top of Everest. I couldn't believe it when I made it. I was utterly elated. Emboldened by my success, I got up the following morning and went on a bit of a skite around Dún Laoghaire with Conor. We had a lovely lunch in a café, nothing fancy, but I was so pleased that I'd made it to this milestone, until I went to get up from the table and couldn't. I didn't have the strength to lift myself up off the chair.

I was a bit embarrassed but smiled at the waitress and made light of it. Then I insisted that Conor take me into Dunnes next to get some things for the children. I bought warm PJs for Ben, and socks and underwear, and as I did, I felt as if I was saying to myself, 'You're back, you're their mother again, you're better. You can do this – you can look after them.' The night before, Ben had been giving out about the quality of his school lunches, so I'd said, 'Right, after school tomorrow, we'll go straight to Aldi and we'll get lunches.' And that's what we did, after lunch and Dunnes. I must have been absolutely mad, but I was high on adrenalin, so thrilled to be back home again, to be able to be Mum again.

When we got home, I did Ben's homework with him and then my wonderful stepmum June Nunn made us toad-in-the-hole for tea. Conor jokingly calls her 'Saint June' because he can't believe anyone could give as much as she does. She never announces her presence, but sometimes I'll come home to find her weeding our front garden; once I pulled up in the car to find her painting our front door! 'It could do with a bit of sprucing up,' was her only explanation. I wanted to hug her – how did she just know what we needed before we did? And her dinners! June is a fantastic cook, to add to her many, many talents, which extend well beyond the domestic sphere – in fact, like my dad, she, too, had served as Dean of the Faculty of Health Science in TCD, although that was years after he had retired. She remains our fount of wisdom on all family health matters. Dad's a very lucky man.

We all sat around and chatted. It was heaven. Who knew that ordinary life could be so fabulous? Then I decided that I'd just have a little sit-down on the armchair, and it suddenly hit me like a ton of bricks – a wave of exhaustion that pinned me to the chair. I could not move. I tried to get up off the seat and I couldn't. I fell over on the floor and then Conor appeared and tried to lift me and because I had surgical stitches, it was so painful. I was crying, 'Oh, my stitches.' It was so awful, but eventually I got up. It's not good for your kids to see you rolling around on the floor, but we got out to the stairs and Conor was holding me from behind, and Lucy was helping too, and I trudged slowly upwards. I got as far as the sitting room and I stayed there for two hours before slinking off, slowly, to bed.

When I woke up the next morning, I realised that it was time to face facts. I wasn't superhuman after all and I needed to ring the hospice, to make preparations and to organise the public health nurse, before we reached crisis levels and it got too difficult for Conor to cope. It was hard, because I knew that making those calls signalled that I was nearing the end of the journey. No one can fight for ever and as I chatted to the hospice nurse, I wondered if I was ready to give up the fight, to surrender. Conor and I talked about when we might need to get a hospital bed into the house and for me to move to the sun room so that I can be close to Conor and the children during the day and so the nurse doesn't have to trudge up three flights of stairs to my bedroom. I wasn't ready for that discussion, even though I knew that it was needed. I wondered what it'd be like to lie there, with no tree to look at, but then I chided myself for being morbid.

As I ponder this, I remember Dad looking after Mum in her final months. He retired early so that he could look after her and he gave her everything. I sometimes think that we weren't fully aware of just how much it took out of him and I wonder if my dying is taking as much out of Conor. I can still remember that Dad used to have her up, showered and dressed before the hospice nurse arrived in the morning and he became an expert cook. He even went out and bought new bed linen, familiarising himself with thread counts and washing instructions, cleaning every day. He was so good to her. He really took it on fully and when Mum died, he was bereft, really. They'd been married for almost forty years, a lifetime of shared love for each other and for us. We were all thrilled when he began a relationship with June, and five years after Mum's death, Dad and June got married. She has been such a kind and steady hand through all of this.

I think I am dying soon, but I'm not going to help it along. I'm not going to say, 'Okay, I'm dying, so I'm going to sit back and read *Hello* magazine, get my feet rubbed and stay in bed.' I'm not saying I'm going to do anything heroic: I know that there'll be no more outings for me, that I probably won't see the sea again, feel the wind in my hair, bump into people on the pier and stop for a chat, but I'm going to get up as much as I can, to be with my family and in my little world for as long as I have left. I've been having lots of visits over the past few months from friends who have always meant so much to me. Not talking about the big stuff, no gushy goodbyes – they know better – but it's been nice to be able to have a laugh and feel their warmth. One of the things that has occurred to me is the idea that the quality of your life can be measured by the people in your life. I am lucky to have such a fabulous group of friends. Kind, funny, thoughtful, interesting people. I don't feel, 'Oh, I'll miss them.' Because they'll still be with me when I go, if that makes any sense. But I'd be very disappointed if they didn't miss me a bit!

When Mum died, she said, 'My life's work is done. My five children were my pride and joy – they and Dad were everything to me and I can say to myself, I had a happy life and I fulfilled my role.' That was all Mum wanted. Now, as I sit here on the sofa, Dougal snoozing beside me, I understand that she was right. I've had a wonderful life, and what I have left now is Conor and Lucy and Ben. I look around the room and my eye is caught by a drawing Lucy did at Christmas of the family: Conor, me, Ben and herself, and Dougal of course. We're all bright colours and big smiles: it's an idealised version of a happy family, but as I look at the drawing of myself with all my hair and my best stripy T-shirt, I know that it's true. We were one big happy family. We *are* one big happy family. In the end, that's all that matters.

CHAPTER 12

PERFECT DAYS AND ENDINGS:
CONOR FERGUSON

I t is Easter Sunday, 12 April 2020. Exactly two months since that awful, beautiful day we said our last goodbye to Keelin. She didn't make it as far as the warm weather, unfortunately, or see the little green buds finally appearing on her tree. She didn't get to finish her story either. So that job falls to me.

She passed away on 8 February 2020, Election Day, and by the strangest of coincidences she was first diagnosed on Election Day 2011. Keelin didn't generally go in for mysticism or marvel at the magic dance of coincidence, but she would have got some perverse enjoyment out of pipping such a significant event to be the lead item on the *Six One News* that evening. *Her* news, as I used to call it. She would have been genuinely overwhelmed by all the messages of sympathy that appeared on her beloved Twitter from the President, Michael D. Higgins, from Taoiseach Leo Varadkar, Fianna Fáil leader Micheál Martin, Sinn Féin's Mary Lou McDonald and many more.

She died in St Vincent's Private Hospital, where the two of us had spent a lot of time together over the preceding six months. She was in and out for chemo and radiotherapy and then she was having falls, so they wanted her in for a few days here and there for that. I began to look forward to those visits, bizarrely enough. It was an oasis of calm when things were going badly, and Dr Janice Walshe had an amazing ability to bring positivity, even when delivering sombre news. She and Keelin had a mutual appreciation thing going on. Keelin trusted her, and moreover they had great chats about each other's outfits. (Janice is a bit of a style icon.)

Keelin had a reputation, among all the doctors and nurses, for never telling them quite how bad she was feeling whenever she was feeling bad. However, coming into January, after a Christmas we thought we would never have, she was pretty straight about the pain that was growing and the breathing that was becoming a worry.

Over the preceding months, I'd often lie there, in the wee small hours, listening to her breathing. Sometimes deep and slow, sometimes laboured or wheezing, or sometimes shallow as if she was awake and thinking. I'd lie there in my own thoughts, wary of saying anything in case she was actually asleep. Or maybe it was something else. I think at some point I became reluctant to get into night-time chats, because they always left me with a sense of looming imminence: something bad was coming. I mean, I *knew* that something bad was coming, obviously, but it was easier to ignore in the daytime or the evening, lying on the bed watching TV together or going back over old photos. But as her breathing got worse, it was now clear again that something bad was coming quite soon.

Only a week previously, I had been in Bologna for the weekend. One of my photos had been selected for a photography exhibition. Looking back now, I feel as if I wasted what would be our second-last weekend together. But there were no omens at the time. Keelin insisted I go. She said she was feeling fine and even the kids said I should go. So I went, and had an interesting time wandering around taking photos in the icy streets where she had lived for a couple of years. It wasn't long after she had returned from there in 1995 that I bumped into her at the Dublin Film Festival Club, in the bar in the Gaiety. We had had a catch-up and a bit of a laugh. It was great to see her again. She had invited me to come along the next day to a film that she was reviewing. I suppose I must have felt something brewing because I bought her a little wooden flute on my way, which she still has. The following weekend she came to my parents' house in Sligo with a couple of friends of mine. We had windswept walks and drank champagne in a cave on the beach, like we were in one of those novels. When she dropped me home that Sunday night, I immediately started missing her, so I gave her a call. Things went from there.

We had known each other for twelve years at this stage and it took a while to get to grips with the fact that – inconceivably – we were now Going Out Together. It was kind of embarrassing. Probably more so for Keelin, because she didn't believe in moving backwards. She had made no secret that she had had a crush on me when she was fifteen or sixteen, and confessed to following me around Grafton Street. But around the same time I started going out with her best friend, so Keelin and I became just-good-friends instead. We saw a lot of each other that first summer. My friends Niall Hadden, Conor O'Brien and I used to call around to her house and listen to the two albums she owned – the Smiths' first album and *Head on the Door* by the Cure – on repeat. She dyed Conor's hair copper and made snarky remarks at me all the while. It took me a long, long time to realise that sometimes female scorn is an expression of something else. It was only when we moved in together a couple of decades later that she showed me the newspaper page she had hung on her teenage bedroom wall. It was from an article in the *Sunday Tribune* about the Dublin 'punk scene' (their words, not mine) and the main photo was a portrait of me. In the margin Keelin had written, in red pen: 'First met in 83'.

So really, by 1995, our brand new boyfriend–girlfriend scenario felt lovely, but more than a little weird for both of us. For the first few weeks she wouldn't even hold my hand in public. I think maybe she was testing me. I don't know. Either way, not so long after that, we moved in together, into a cool art deco-style apartment building that sits amid a Georgian terrace near the top of Pembroke Street. My sister Ciara had been living there and was moving out. I couldn't believe it when Keelin suggested that we move in together. I had always liked having my own space, but for the first time in my life I was able to look into the future and see what the rest of my life might possibly look like. And it looked very nice.

It was a halcyon time. My career in advertising was going really well and Keelin had progressed quickly from doing movie reviews on *12 to 1* to co-presenting *Black Box*, RTÉ's vibrant new arts show. We regularly agreed on how lucky we were. 'A bit too lucky,' I used to say, to her great perplexity. 'Like, if you saw us as a couple in a film, you'd think, look at this pair all lovey-dovey. Something *bad* is going to happen to them.' But for a long time nothing did.

❧

When I returned from Bologna, I could see that Keelin was tired after the weekend. We talked about her memories of the city and started toying with plans for our twentieth wedding anniversary, which was now just a few days away. Inevitably we got talking about the wedding day, 29 January 2000. It had been a long time coming. Keelin always said how much she had loved the idea of getting married as a child – her first Holy Communion was 'a practice run'. The topic seemed to be coming up regularly. But I just ... wasn't ... quite ... ready ... yet. It was that whole thing of being the centre of attention for an entire day. Keelin was growing frustrated at my failure to engage. One day I said to her, 'The problem is *you* keep bringing it up all the time. So I never have long enough to make up my own mind.'

So she stopped mentioning it, and lo and behold, suddenly it felt like a great idea. The slightly disastrous marriage proposal in Colombia followed, and sometime after that she chose her engagement and wedding rings in an antique shop in the Powerscourt Centre. Keelin liked nice things but generally baulked at spending what she would call 'unnecessary' sums of money, and I felt the same way, as long as she was happy. So the engagement ring was modest enough, but for her wedding ring she picked a lovely piece with a band of diamonds across the top. She loved it, but it used to irritate her skin, so sometimes she kept it in her pocket. That's how, one New Year's Eve on Camden Street, she accidentally tossed it into the cup of a homeless man, along with some change. She never got it back, in spite of Miriam O'Callaghan very kindly featuring it on her radio show. It's just stuff anyway, and Keelin's attitude was always, 'If I can do something about it, I'll do all I possibly can. But if I can't do anything, I'll park it and move on.' It was this incredibly pragmatic attitude that helped her throughout her career and her experience with cancer.

If Keelin stood out as a broadcaster, in my opinion it was because she was a bit different. Not in a kooky or ostentatious way, but instinctively; and she wanted our wedding to be a bit different too. A wet winter wedding was not a problem for her. I had deejayed at a wedding in Markree Castle, County Sligo, a couple of years previously and Keelin had been invited along. She had set her heart on it then, even though – as her mum pointed out – some of the splendid neo-Gothic windows seemed to be held together with Sellotape and there was an empty Cadet bottle sitting on top of the curtains in the dining room. Keelin didn't care: it was perfect. (Even though the boiler packed it in on the morning of the wedding, meaning cold showers all round. Apart from the bride, who had one in the make-up artist's house.)

But before all that we had the small matter of getting our wedding outfits made within the three weeks that remained between Christmas and the big day. Keelin didn't want to go down the great white bride route, instead opting for a wide layered skirt in taupe satin and tulle, which her friend Deborah's auntie ran up for her. She would wear this with a simple white cashmere wrap-over cardigan and vintage diamond earrings. She looked amazing, with her hair all Grace Kellyed up. Understated and glamorous at the same time. I had set my heart on a deep red corduroy suit. The woman in the shop where I bought the material recommended a tailor who, it transpired, was a bit fond of the bottle. I went for a fitting once and found him asleep with his head on an ironing board and a Guinness bottle top on the floor. I had to stress to him, after gently rousing him, how critical it was that the suit be ready in time. Because when else was I going to get to dress up in a flaming red suit?

We had found a gorgeous, tiny church just outside Sligo town, with a kind and forbearing priest who didn't seem to mind that one of the readings – about how unlikely it is, given our infinite universe, for atoms to gather and form into two people who then meet and fall in love – was written by radical atheist Richard Dawkins. Father Jim was more concerned that, without the Mass, it was going to be over very quickly and should we maybe 'pad it out' a bit? I had picked an instrumental piano piece from David Lynch's film *Wild at Heart* to play as Keelin and Derry walked up the aisle. It was a short aisle, so I thought the track would be long enough at two minutes and twenty seconds. The only problem was, just as Keelin arrived at the door, she had to wait for some last-minute guests to bundle themselves in. Meanwhile, I was at the altar thinking, 'Hurry up, you're going to run out of music and be walking up the aisle in silence.' But luckily she appeared just in time, looking phenomenal. It was a lovely ceremony. We kissed, then went to sign the register as 'Perfect Day' by Lou Reed played in the background. It was a song I had always found moving. A simple, almost naive lyric shot through with a couple of lines of darkness. Yin and yang, which is how we were.

In the early years of our relationship, I used to tell Keelin that she loved me 'about fifteen per cent too much'. I just didn't feel I entirely deserved the level of attention she gave me. Anyway, things changed when we had children. The fascination shifted over. The early bit of having a baby was lovely and enhanced our sense of togetherness, especially after the anxiety of first a miscarriage, then a protracted failure to conceive, then the rather unsexy but ultimately miraculous business of IVF. Keelin was besotted with Lucy. But the three-in-a-bed lark that took hold was far from ideal. And then Ben came along and he was a stunner too, switching with Lucy to occupy the middle space in the bed for a number of years ... So the 'love percentage' fluctuated, and there were lengthy times when it felt like at least fifteen per cent too little. I suppose she wanted to give so much to her children, her career *and* her marriage – and there's only so much to give.

But most of the time, she was extremely loving and loveable; a wonderful, enthusiastic, endlessly curious, confoundingly inconsistent but never dull or lazy-minded person. She loved to see others succeed, and she would bombard you with questions and advice; often unsolicited, sometimes unwanted, but always well-meaning and smart. I certainly relied on her frank opinions at times – like a cold splash of water to the face, bringing me to my senses, or a lifebelt helping me swim closer to my own ambitions.

We enjoyed each other's company in a way that not all couples do. At social occasions, when the wider group divided inevitably into The Men and The Women, I used to love it when she'd sidle up next to me and join the conversation, or look at me as if I was still the interesting, surprising person she'd found me to be in our late twenties. In a marriage, sometimes you can get lost amid the busyness of days: the school runs and domestic necessities, the differences in parenting policy and the practical minutiae. The language of married life tends towards, 'Don't forget to buy toilet rolls ... I don't suppose you hung out the wet sheets … So it's *my* turn to cook again? … I thought you said that the kids should go to bed early tonight …' An edge creeps in, a certain weariness at the same joke being cracked *again*, a cute mannerism long gone stale. We were no exception to this process. However, I think maybe it was the differences between us, in terms of personality and outlook, that engaged us with each other so well, between the squabbles. Certainly, I was fascinated by her foibles and contradictions. Although she sometimes seemed to feel like the butt of the joke whenever I chortled at some quintessentially Keelinesque thing she said or did. And I too would often be hurt by the possibility that, some of the time, she might find me tiresome, irritating or negative.

I wonder is this just how married life *is*, in middle age? When you know someone so well, it's hard not to take it all for granted. You feel assured that the romantic spirit of your early years will continue to glow like embers under the growing pile of ashes that life creates. But it takes work to reconcile the different needs that arise in a relationship. It takes more than just love; it takes a combination of flexibility and staying power. For instance, Keelin liked change. Well, not change, actually – *progress*. She wasn't avaricious or hugely aspirational. She was genuinely grateful for what we had, but sometime in the new year of 2016 she started to feel that her career was meandering a bit and she began looking for something else to aim for, a new project to lead us onward. It was her nature. And it was my nature to say, Sure we're probably grand how we are for the moment. But deep down I knew that we were on the move.

When we were due to come home from Paris in late 2002, I told her firmly, possibly with my finger outstretched, 'We're not going looking for a new house as soon as we get home, right? We'll stay in Rialto for a while and get our bearings.' She left Paris that October, and by the time I joined her in Dublin at Christmas, she had found what was to be our next home, near Leonard's Corner on South Circular Road. It was a late-Victorian terrace that had been carved up into five flats that needed six months' work. We had the money and patience for four. We had a great life in that house. We raised Lucy and Ben there. They got such great joy out of the garden and the trampoline that was big enough to take all of us. Memories of sitting out with friends late on a summer evening, or lounging in deckchairs with a glass of rosé and unread newspapers on our laps. My bedtime story sessions were interminable; Keelin took a more abbreviated approach ('Mama, you skipped the big bit in the middle!'). Apart from that, she gave our children everything. I used to think she was like an all-American mom from the fifties – so sweet and enthusiastic with her little angels – and they were! She was very protective, but as they grew, she was the one who gave them more freedom to explore and fall over and learn to pick themselves up again. We shared the parenting, but without doubt, Keelin's instincts did more to help them grow in resilience and strength.

At the same time, she was building up a fantastic body of work in her career. Looking back at it, as we did in the last several months, I was reminded of the comment Keelin made often about broadcasting: you need to take yourself out of the equation. And it's true, I would frequently think – where is she? She was hardly ever on camera, because she believed the story should be told by the people in it, the camera there to observe their experiences. She didn't think people tuned in to see her, but I bet some of them did. I did, anyway. Her reports were always well-written, hard-hitting, and she understood the value of incisive editing, but also, to me, her face was a lovely interruption during all those tales of woe.

We had lots of dinner parties, celebrations and toasts to dear departed in that house. Keelin's mum died while we were living there; my dad Vincent and brother Johnny did too. The comfort of a family home amounts to more than just soft furnishings – there's the soothing ache of the memories it contains. But by 2015, Keelin had found a new plan. She'd had enough of city-centre living and yearned to be near the sea where we had both grown up, and to be closer to the families we had grown up with. So we started looking at houses in the Dún Laoghaire area. It was spring and the blossoms were out and Keelin dragged me along to see a couple of houses that had potential, but just weren't quite right. For a laugh, we had a look at a beautiful terraced house overlooking a park. We were mainly being nosy, because in the few photos we saw it looked intriguing and one of the rooms had this amazing wallpaper. It turned out to be a bit of a wreck, though – holes in the roof, collapsing plasterwork, dodgy electrics galore – a project that was way beyond our budget. But, somehow, we bought it.

We sat down with our builder, Warren. He had done great work on our old house, only two years previously, and he and his men always seemed to enjoy the chats with Keelin because she was full of mad ideas and enthusiasm. (My role was more to think things through and mutter, 'That's a crazy idea' every now and then. And trying to keep the children or the dog from getting injured by all the sharp objects and falling masonry.) Warren reckoned the job of refurbishing the new house would take a good six months. Meanwhile, we decided we could live out of boxes in one room plus a very dodgy kitchen for a while, couldn't we? At this stage Keelin was working on *Morning Ireland*, which was proper hard work. Up at 4.30 a.m., home by 10 a.m., but then staying on top of the news all day: the *Six One*, *Channel 4 News*, the *Nine O'Clock News*, *Newsnight*, Twitter. She loved being around for the kids in the afternoon and hanging out in the park, but come September, life was getting difficult. The rickety windows were no match for the wind and it increasingly felt like we were living in a haunted house – along with mice and some pigeons who used to frequently drop by. It was during all this that Keelin started experiencing the nagging pain in her back. She went for tests and our lives took an even more dramatic swerve into the unknown.

When the cancer was first diagnosed in 2011 and we had gone to Kelly's Hotel in Rosslare, I remember taking photos of Keelin and the kids on the beach and thinking, This could be the last time we do anything like this. Thankfully, I was catastrophising unneces sarily and we got to do lots of good stuff, but I found it hard to permanently shake the idea that the cancer might still be out there beyond the horizon.

After the second diagnosis we kept the infor-mation close, mentioning it to people as the need or opportunity arose. Keelin didn't want everyone knowing at the same time. Indeed, as conversa-tions about the possibility of the *Six One* job were gathering momentum, it was important that she had some control over exactly who knew what. But from the people who did know, the help came in hot and fast. In a kitchen that could barely contain us, we wrangled the shepherd's pies, curries, lasagnes and wheatgrass we were given. The kindness meant a lot because at this stage we were renting a house just up the road. It was cold, Christmas was coming and the building was still waiting to begin. We visited the house regularly, and every time, the same thought returned to me: 'We are *so* fucked.'

But the new year came around. Keelin's treatment started. The kids settled into their new school. The building started. That Easter, we had to leave the rented house because the owners wanted to put it on the market. We were sort of couch-surfing, relying on the kindness of friends and Derry and June for a few weeks until we could move back in. When we did, it was all four of us, plus the dog, sleeping, eating, working, watching TV in the one room – while the building work continued around us. That was Keelin's way of doing things and I went along with it because the whole crazy, incredibly dusty situation was a distraction from what was really going on.

By the following Christmas, the house was transformed, and Keelin was determined to enjoy it. In between the trips to St Vincent's and the different treatments that went on, we had a big housewarming party that February. The house was thronged, there was dancing and Liam Ó Maonlaí played the piano so hard a few glasses danced off the edge onto the floor. We had dinner parties, lunches, even the odd picnic in the park. We weren't going to give up living. Keelin's energy levels fluctuated, but she went on working. She didn't lose her hair until the very end. In fact, she looked amazing throughout. Very few people knew she was ill, and you wouldn't have guessed it to see her dancing at our friend Paul's fiftieth birthday party in Lucca, Italy or mingling at the last, admittedly scaled-down, soirée we had for my birthday last November.

She didn't really like to characterise her situation as a *battle* with cancer – even though that's what it was. She knew premature death was inevitable, but nobody knew *how long* we had left. The plan was to keep on pushing until there was no longer a choice in the matter. So she took ownership of it, she did her research, she kept despair at bay. I always found it easier to put my trust in her than to resist her. That's how come we ended up on our last adventure: flying to the NIH to apply for treatment.

To me, our journey across the sea felt like a second honeymoon. Due to a conspiracy of kindness conducted by her old Loreto gang, we ended up in the private terminal at Dublin airport, where we got the whole Bono treatment. A car drove us to Customs, where a wheelchair was waiting for Keelin. At this stage she was walking with a stick generally, but it was handy to have the wheels in a busy airport. On the plane we were ushered to the front row in first class! Not only that, but the pilot, Elaine Egan, had been in Keelin's class in school. I took a photo of the two of them together, and then the steward took a photo of the two of us, champagne glasses in hand, looking like a slightly less classy version of Elizabeth Taylor and Richard Burton.

For the first while it was a bit of a thrill to be in America. We got to wander the streets and see the buildings: the FBI Headquarters, the Department of Justice, the Department of Homeland Security, the Capitol, the White House. Thanks to Miriam O'Callaghan, we got invited to the Irish Ambassador's residence for tea. We even took a train to Baltimore, where *The Wire* was based – had a little stroll, ate a little lobster and then got the train back to DC. It was just us again, but it was slow going. Looking back, I wonder was Keelin pushing herself too hard for my benefit? And was I looking after her enough? I kept suggesting we get taxis, but she said she enjoyed the freedom of walking around. She said she liked the simplicity of our days then; it was a break from reality, in a way, from having to talk to anyone or deal with anything. But ten days turned into three weeks. We missed being there for Lucy's last day in primary school, her first disco – it felt quite disempowering for Keelin, I think, to be missing key moments where only a mother will do: getting emotional at the school gates; helping Lucy choose an outfit; and giving counsel on the ways of the disco. Luckily, our Lucy managed just fine with the help of her Auntie Emma.

The medics in the NIH seemed to fall for Keelin's charms. Because she wasn't precious or demanding – she was engaged and asked informed questions. It had taken a lot of tenacity to get here and she was determined to assure them that she was a healthy candidate. (She even told me to hide her stick – she didn't want them to know that she needed it.)

After a couple of days of tests, they told Keelin that she had been accepted onto the programme. They would need us to return to the US probably within the next few months to begin treatment and we'd have to stay there for up to six months after that. Keelin was so thrilled. My own feelings were more mixed: how would we manage the children – should they move to the US with us or stay in their normal lives? Where would we live? But mostly: if she has to come off chemo and endure the treatment – which involves 'turning off' the patient's auto-immune system for a while, leaving them perilously sensitive to even the most minor infection – might it all prove too much for her body? Already, I could see her condition was getting worse. She was starting to lose her appetite. At that point, all she craved was a steady supply of ice pops. I remember going to get her one from the freezer on the ward, thinking, What if we come back and she ends up dying here, three thousand miles from home?

The quest to complete the treatment in the US was Keelin's last big project. And the only one that didn't succeed. Now there was no hope, just the burning question of how long. We had experienced plenty of twists and turns along the road, but – if I may persist with the analogy – there were also plenty of smooth, scenic stretches too; times on cruise-control when it hardly felt we were moving at all, cresting hills to discover beautiful panoramas stretched out and waiting.

But coming towards the end, life was just getting harder for her to enjoy. I wouldn't say either of us felt the emotional pain we expected and feared all along, the anguish. Maybe that pain gets released later. Breaking the news to children, parents, siblings, friends was hard, but everyone was brilliant, dealing with it just as Keelin herself wanted it to be dealt with – no dramatics or bitterness, just a calm accep tance. Or at least, that's how it seemed anyway. Keelin used to say that I knew her better than she knew herself. But there were many times, as I have discovered reading this book, when she held back her true feelings or made more of an effort than perhaps she needed to, for the benefit of me or the children. She had a gift for staying in the moment – and keeping us in that moment with her. I'm so grateful to her for that. For that and so many other things. She was a doer. She made things happen, even in the last six months. Like a boat trip on the Shannon in the last days of summer, which was something she had always wanted to do. She says she didn't have a bucket list, but there was that; our last lunch in

Cavistons in Glasthule; and the job of moving our laundry room to the top of the house – 'You'll thank me for this when I'm gone,' she said. She just loved to have a mission. Only a few weeks before she went, she insisted on a visit to Shaws ('Almost nationwide!') to see if they had any bargains on bed linen. At this stage she needed a wheelchair if she was going more than twenty metres, and their bedding department is in the basement. Nevertheless, Keelin remained undaunted. She asked the security guard to keep an eye on her wheelchair and she walked downstairs on my arm, where the women behind the counter were delighted to see her again, all smiles and chat.

I realise that this heroic pursuit of something as mundane as bed sheets probably sits slightly askew of the common perception that Keelin was fancy or sophisticated. She was a bit of that too, but she was mostly practical and no-nonsense. And if she wanted to peruse the 100% cotton bedsheets, by golly she would!

The days got simpler. We spent many, many hours lying on our bed at the top of the house, but we never made it to the end of *The Sopranos*. She went into hospital on the Monday after our wedding anniversary. She was still getting treatment, but was growing increasingly unsteady. It was made clear to us that we were on a steep downward incline. Keelin continued being visited by the ones she loved most, right up until the last hours; until finally she slipped away peacefully, with the warm sun on her face, and Lucy, Ben and me around her. Just us and all the love. The hospital placed a blue butterfly on her door. The clouds came and a storm followed soon after.

EPILOGUE

Keelin went while the going was good – just before the Covid-19 pandemic marched in and turned the world upside-down. It's a big consolation, in a way, that she's not around for it. She would have been disturbed and fascinated in equal measure, I think. The intricacies of it would have fascinated her. She liked the way science works, a bit like journalism, deriving certainties out of the unknown. She told me she found genuine comfort in the natural order of things, the circle of life. Like the tree that provides oxygen, shelter and shade year after year, for as long as it possibly can, and then quietly stops.

It's hard not to feel guilty, living on in her wake. The weather has warmed up. It's almost like life has moved on. Our bereavement was quickly displaced by the new world of coronavirus. I have plenty of time on my hands to consider any misdemeanours or unkindnesses I may have done over the years. The petty arguments and mean words, the times when she may have needed more support than it occurred to me to give; the times when I thought, You look gorgeous, but didn't say it. And it's hard to shake the feeling that I held Keelin back in some ways: as someone who liked to keep moving forward, I know she would have married, mortgaged and had children sooner were it not for my ponderous, hesitant ways.

One thing I had fixed in my mind was that her funeral would be one worth going to. She was clear that she wanted it to be personal and real. Not too formal or too mournful, and with a few laughs thrown in. She was intrigued about who might turn up and would have been shocked to see such a large and stellar turnout (including a long-lost ex who came over from London). She never would have believed that her death could have affected people so much. We talked about music. We didn't really have 'our song', as such. 'Protection' by Massive Attack and 'Missing' by Everything But the Girl had felt 'significant' for us, but kind of *too* poignant now. There were plenty of numbers that we had jumped about to over the years, but none of them would have been quite right. Songs from our youth had maybe belonged more to other relationships. I suggested 'This Is the Sea' by the Waterboys and she liked that, not so much because of the Waterboys or because the song has such a powerful message about life and change, but simply because she loved the sea! It always lifted her. Whether it was the roar of the waves at Keem in Achill, the regal expanse of Rosses Point in Sligo or the body-shocking, life-affirming embrace of the Forty Foot, she was entranced by it. I have so many photos of her walking on beaches, always from behind. I'd have stopped to take a photo of the waves; I'd turn around to say, 'That was a good one,' and she'd be already gone, marching away up the beach.

For the end-of-funeral song, we were stuck. 'What about "There Is A Light That Never Goes Out" by The Smiths?' I asked. That's what I had written on the card for our wedding anniversary: 'You are the light that will never go out.'

'Oh, I thought you'd made up that line,' she said, disappointed.

'Eh, no. Morrissey got there first. But it's still true.'

She held my hand. 'How does it go again?'

So I sang a bit of the song for her and we both stared at the ceiling, musing on Morrissey's romantic poignancy and abject miserabilism. And on how much change the years can bring. We both could have burst into tears, but we burst out laughing instead. And we moved on.

'We could go with "Perfect Day" by Lou Reed?' I said.

'Yes, I know who wrote it! But is that not a bit inappropriate? It's hardly a perfect day!' But I reminded her it had been the main song in the church at our wedding. 'Oh, yeah. That would be lovely.' We discussed who might sing on the day. We knew we could rely on Liam Ó Maonlaí to do the honours, and I asked him could he round up Fiachna Ó Braonáin and Julie Feeney, who Keelin had met on the radio and really liked. She had asked if Steve Wall might sing as well, and he said he'd love to. Between them they gave us a rendition of the song that seemed to bring everyone together, from the President and Taoiseach to the kids from the Harold School and Loreto Abbey Dalkey, from the heads of charities and representatives from Keelin's beloved Irish Book Awards, to the trainers from Lucy's Cuala GAA team, and of course the family and friends who would miss her the most. We all filed out of the church into the cold, blue-skied day as the church bells were ringing a merry, spring-like tune. She didn't want deathly bongs, and this wasn't that. Just marking her passing with a nod, an ache and a smile.

ACKNOWLEDGEMENTS

On behalf of Keelin, Lucy, Ben and Conor:

Many thanks to our great friends Niamh O'Connor and Nicola Byrne for helping to instigate this book; to the wonderful Alison Walsh, whom Keelin trusted to assemble her story; to Deirdre Nolan, Teresa Daly and all the team at Gill Books, who have done a brilliant job in difficult circumstances; and to Marianne Gunn O'Connor for her incredible kindness and support throughout.

This book wouldn't have been possible without the amazing people who cared for Keelin during her final months. Thanks to Dr Janice Walshe and all at St Vincent's Private Hospital, particularly the nurses (and hospitality) on Cedar Ward, who were so nice over the last few years; to Professor John Armstrong and the radiotherapy department; to the doctors and nurses in Palliative Care; to the fantastic home-visiting team from Our Lady's Hospice, Blackrock; and to ARC Cancer Support Centre.

In RTÉ, huge thanks to Hilary McGouran, Jon Williams, Caitríona Perry, Dee Forbes, Declan McBennett and Tanya McNulty for your immense support; and to Noel Curran, Ed Mulhall and Kevin Bakhurst, ex-RTÉ; to Sean Mac Giolla Phadraig for his help with this book; to the RTÉ hair and make-up and wardrobe departments (especially Catherine Manning, who visited Keelin in her last days to help her choose a good funeral outfit!).

Thanks to the Loreto Girls, to Judy Kelly, Louise Webb and all our friends.

Finally, our endless gratitude to the Shanley and Ferguson families – especially Derry Shanley, June Nunn and Noeleen Ferguson.

NUJ
NATIONAL UNION of JOURNALISTS

PRESS

NAME KEELIN SHANLEY

UNION NO. 92692

EXPIRES: 31ST DECEMBER 2003